Taking Control of Your Teaching Career

A guide for teachers

John Howson

Routledge
Taylor & Francis Group

LONDON AND NEW YORK

the TES

371.102
HOW

First published 2007 by Routledge
2 Park Square, Milton Park, Abingdon OX14 4RN

Simultaneously published in the USA and Canada
by Routledge
270 Madison Avenue, New York, NY 10016

*Routledge is an imprint of the Taylor & Francis Group,
an informa business*

© 2007 John Howson

Typeset in Times New Roman by
Greengate Publishing Services, Tonbridge, Kent
Printed and bound in Great Britain by
Cromwell Press, Trowbridge, Wiltshire

British Library Cataloguing in Publication Data
A catalogue record for this book is available from the British Library

Library of Congress Cataloging in Publication Data
Howson, John.
Taking control of your teaching career / John Howson. – 1st ed.
    p. cm.
Includes bibliographical references and index.
1. Teaching–Vocational guidance–Great Britain. I. Title.

LB1775.4.H69 2007
371.10023–dc22

2006022002

ISBN10 0–415–34435–2 (pbk)   ISBN13 978–0–415–34435–7 (pbk)
ISBN10 0–203–96623–6 (ebk)   ISBN13 978–0–203–96623–5 (ebk)

Taking Control of Your Teaching Career

There are over 400,000 teachers working in schools in England and Wales. *Taking Control of Your Teaching Career* is designed to help them take charge of their careers and put themselves in the driving seat.

Based upon John Howson's popular column in *The Times Educational Supplement*, the book outlines the possible career options open to teachers who:

- have just finished their Induction Year;
- are considering taking on a leadership role;
- are looking to take time out of the classroom; or
- want to come back to teaching.

Taking Control of Your Teaching Career is arranged in chapters based on the decisions teachers will make, from after qualifying to retirement. Each chapter of this practical guide answers real questions from the author's column, giving guidance to teachers at every stage of their career.

The book seeks to provide advice in an easily accessible manner that avoids the stuffy prose of many career guidance manuals. It reflects the fact that teachers need to take charge of their careers if they are not to risk being left to their fate.

John Howson is Director of Education Data Surveys; Visiting Professor at Oxford Brookes University; Visiting Senior Research Fellow at Oxford University; and former Deputy Head, School of Education at Oxford Brookes University.

Contents

Illustrations

Figures

Tables

Preface

Each year, in England, around 40,000 people embark on a journey that will lead them towards becoming a teacher. There are also others who train in Wales, Scotland or Northern Ireland. They are intending to join a profession that currently employs nearly half a million people. Throughout England, there are also nearly as many qualified teachers who are not currently employed in schools. Some work in other educational settings as anything from a psychologist to a Chief Education Officer, or a poet to a play group leader. Others are taking time out to travel, raise a family or just to pursue other interests. Each year, some who have left the profession will also seek to return, sometimes part-time, sometimes full-time.

With such a large and diverse workforce, teaching can provide a variety of different career paths. Unlike working for many large organisations, where rigid promotion policies are often geared to appraisal reports from your superior, teaching can offer individuals the chance to take control of their career at every stage. This is not to deny that luck doesn't play a part; it certainly has on a couple of occasions in my own career. But in one sense everyone makes their own luck. This is where knowing how to take control of your career is important.

Sadly, too often teachers at all stages of their lives are left without a route map to help them decide on the next move; when and what should it be? For those who are content to take what life has to offer, this isn't a problem. That is unless, or until, they hit a snag. They may suddenly discover that, for instance, because of falling rolls, their school has to shed a teacher, and they are in the frame for redundancy. As the school population drops steadily over the next few years this may be a more common event than many teachers realise. Alternatively, after many happy and fulfilling years teaching, their school appoints a new head. The new regime may be different from the old one; should they adapt or look for something different?

The idea for this book had its genesis in one of the weekly columns that I have written over the years for *The Times Educational Supplement.* Teachers, along with other readers, have been regularly writing and emailing me, seeking advice about their careers. It is clear that many either don't know where else to turn to, or maybe just want a second opinion.

In the past few years the importance of good professional development for the teaching profession has once again been recognised by the government. This is good news for all teachers, but the needs of schools and the needs of an individual may not always be the same. Good career development is more than amassing just a collection of courses. It needs a focus that is designed to offer the chance for an individual to move forward along their chosen career path.

This book is designed to offer some advice. It is structured in a broadly chronological fashion, and starts after the end of the Induction Year, when a teacher has become fully qualified. It ends with some thoughts about the future of the profession, since those teachers who are currently in the early years of their careers can expect still to be working almost up to the middle of the century. Who knows what the pattern of education will look like by then? However, we can be certain that it will still require dedicated professionals, for learning, though personal, is a very social activity for most people, especially during childhood and adolescence. However, this isn't a recipe book: it isn't a 'follow these instructions and you will end up as a head teacher'. I don't believe that is how careers should operate. In the end, everyone has to take responsibility for their own careers. I can only offer advice and suggestions.

This book would not have been written without the aid of the hundreds of teachers, and would-be teachers, who have written in with their queries over the years. I hope that my advice has been helpful. To all who read this book, good luck with your career.

John Howson
Oxford, 2006

1 After the Induction Year

This chapter looks at some of the issues that arise in the years immediately after the end of the Induction Year. At this time, many teachers confront decisions about when to change schools, how soon it is appropriate to accept additional responsibilities, and even whether they want to stay in the profession. There is in fact a significant loss to the profession of teachers in their first three years, and it seems that many do not return. This is also the point at which it is wise to consider a career plan. Talk with more experienced colleagues about the sorts of options that are open to you now and in both the medium and longer terms. Try to review these options at regular intervals. Do not bother to wait for an appraisal; it is your career and you should be prepared to be in the driving seat.

I have passed my Induction Year. Am I a fully fledged teacher now?

Once you have passed your Induction Year, you can relax and enjoy your new-found status as a fully qualified professional, so long as you keep up your registration with the General Teaching Council. However, being a professional has responsibilities as well as rewards. Professionals have a duty to keep up to date with their professional knowledge, and teachers are no different in this respect from other professionals they encounter in their own lives. Teachers expect their doctors to be able to know the best way of dealing with their ailments, and dentists to be up to date with developments in dental technology and pain relief. Similarly, parents have a right to expect that teachers will keep abreast of developments in subject knowledge, teaching practices and whatever other skills they need to remain accomplished professionals.

Just because you passed your Induction Year, that doesn't mean that you now know everything. Each class and year group is different from the one that went before. Look on your second year as one of consolidation. You may discover that what worked the first year doesn't always work second time around, and there are those bits that didn't work at all last year and will certainly need revising. Even though you won't have a mentor this year, and you will, for the first time, have to teach a full timetable, still try to find time to ask questions. If your school has a staff development policy in place and, perhaps, has Investor in People status, you should try to arrange for time to watch others teach.

I have just completed my year as an NQT [newly qualified teacher] in a lovely school. I am enjoying teaching but there does not seem to be much opportunity for promotion. How long should I stay in the school before seeking a new post?

There is no easy answer to this question. If you are going for promotion because you need the money, perhaps because you want to start saving for a deposit on a property, beware of taking on too much responsibility too soon. Have you discussed the issue with the person who was your mentor last year, or with those you work with? In the end, the decision will have to be a personal one. You will have to decide whether the fact that the school where you are at present is, in your own words, 'lovely', outweighs the fact that you might be more likely to receive an early promotion at another school.

I have just started teaching in a school that is shrinking in size. Does anyone know what percentage of older teachers will be retiring in the near future, and how it will affect my job prospects? The town I'm currently in has tens of applications for just one job.

About 100,000 teachers in England are over 50; that's approaching a third of the active teaching force. So, there will be lots of retirements over the next decade. However, as you point out, schools – and especially secondary schools – will be facing a period of falling rolls. This will cut the school population, even if no pupils transfer to the further education sector for part of their studies. On balance, there will be plenty of posts for middle management, but possibly fewer posts for new entrants. One other note on the job front: there are more posts due to teachers in their thirties taking maternity leave; however, these are usually only temporary positions.

I have been teaching for just a year but my head of department has left and it has been suggested that I take over, at least in the short term. Is this a good idea?

Probably not. Do you have enough experience to take on the role? If it was just the two of you, some parts of the job might not be too difficult, but how would you feel if an NQT was appointed to the other post and you were responsible for mentoring them, despite having only a year's teaching experience yourself? If you are teaching in an area that traditionally has recruitment problems, it might seem to both the head and yourself that taking on the post was the lesser of two evils. However, the danger is that once you have agreed to do the job, no further help may be forthcoming. This is something you will have to assess by looking at what happens in your school. Are staff generally well supported, or are they too often left to their own devices? What arrangements are made for staff development to cover both the leadership and administrative elements of a head of department's role? With health and safety and budget management just two of the elements that comprise the role of a modern head of department, do you really want to take on this responsibility without any training?

I have been at my present school for three years, since I finished my training. Is it time to move on?

Why do you have itchy feet at this point? Is it because you think that a move will bring new challenges? This is often the reason for a move. Teachers feel that they can make a fresh start by moving to a new school and will have learnt from their mistakes. Certainly it is possible to widen your horizons by a move, especially if you choose a school with a different type of focus. Perhaps you can move to one that has more parental involvement or a wider range of before- and after-school activities. Of course, you will face the challenge of adapting to the new circumstances and learning afresh all the things that you currently take for granted – not least the micro-politics of the school, and the staffroom culture.

Are there any advantages to staying put, or will you be seen as a stick-in-the-mud in career terms? In the secondary sector, you can always argue that it is good to see a whole cohort through from entry from primary school until they leave five or even seven years later. Whichever sector you teach in, there is the possibility of measuring whether you are doing better with each successive year you spend in the school – and if not, why not?

Moving too frequently may make you look like something of a gadfly with no staying power. This won't matter at the start of your career, but may be something you will need to be able to justify at interview after a few quick moves. In the end, the final decision to move is when it feels right for you. Factors to consider will include not only your career but also how your teaching fits in with the rest of your life.

How should I view the various stages of my career?

It may be worth dividing your future career into three. These three parts can be described respectively as your goals, aims and aspirations. Goals are what you want to do in the near future, aims your medium-term ambitions and aspirations the career direction you want to work towards. Obviously, ambitions and aspirations can be fluid, as opportunities you haven't considered may arise in the course of your working life. For instance, those of us who started teaching in the early 1970s could hardly have guessed at the effects of the IT revolution, and the opportunities that it could create.

However, all this is in the future. You are currently considering when to make a move from your present post. The job market in teaching is just that, a mixture of buyers and sellers. Buyers – that is, schools – will be looking for staff with a mixture of experience, knowledge and enthusiasm. Sellers – that is, people like yourself – will be looking for jobs that provide satisfaction, career development opportunities, and financial and other intrinsic benefits, such as a good working environment.

Where there are lots of sellers – that is, when the job proves popular – schools can pick and choose; but if there are few people interested in applying, or able to apply, for a post, then schools may need to adjust what is on offer to attract more interest. This is often achieved for more senior posts through paying more, but it can be done in other ways as well.

If you have a career plan, you will avoid being enticed into applying for posts before you are ready for them. On the other hand, you won't leave it so long that you are not as attractive an appointee as others applying for the post at the same time as yourself.

This means that you should look at what schools advertising the kinds of posts you are interested in applying for are putting in their adverts in the *TES*. Send off for details of some posts, so that you can get a feel for the person specifications, and match your experience against what is required. If necessary, work on your personal development plan so that you can meet what is required, and then start applying. You may be lucky first time, but you may need several goes before you find a job that you want, and a school finds you are the person that they have been looking for.

Finally, good teachers recognise the anguish that the thought of leaving their present post causes. What will happen to the pupils that you are currently teaching? All teachers have to face up to this dilemma at some point in their careers. You will just have to trust that your successor will do as good a job as you did; or possibly an even better one.

I want to go on a course that I think will benefit my career. Should I expect the school to pay?

This is a tricky question. Seen from the perspective of a head teacher with a tight budget, money spent on staff development that doesn't meet the school's immediate needs feels like a waste of precious resources. However, if every head took that line there would be little career development. Personally, I believe that a good school should recognise that one of the reasons staff will want to work there is that the school looks after their needs. In doing so, it also looks after the needs of its pupils. So there is both a marketing case – attracting new staff – and an educational case – better-qualified teachers – for persuading head teachers and staff development committees that some money should be spent on helping staff acquire the expertise to be able to move on to other jobs, either in the same school or elsewhere.

But remember, funds for staff development are always under pressure and are rarely sufficient to meet all the claims there are on the budget, so expect to make some investment yourself. This can be financial or it can be by selecting activities that run in your own time, so that no supply cover is needed.

I did a general primary course that covered the age range from 5 to 11 and have taught a Key Stage 2 class for the past two years. I have seen a post for a Reception class teacher that interests me. Can I apply?

In theory, the answer is yes, but do you feel equipped for such a change in direction? There is a lot of difference between teaching a Reception class and teaching at Key Stage 2, even though they are both in the primary sector. Why do you want to make the change? Have you arranged to spend any time in a Reception class to check out whether it is really for you? If you are convinced that you want to make the change, it will strengthen any application you make if you can show that you have been undertaking professional development to equip you for teaching the younger age group. You could approach the early years adviser in your local authority for advice and guidance about your possible career move.

I qualified as an ICT teacher in my late forties, about five years ago. I'm still trying to find a job.

For my NQT year I worked away from home in the South East. At the end of the year, I was informed that they'd only needed me for an Ofsted inspection. I'd wasted all the usual costs trying to buy a house and on bed and breakfast accommodation.

For the next year I was a temporary ICT co-ordinator in a secondary school within driving distance of home. I set everything up from scratch. At the end of that year, I was told they were teaching ICT via a GNVQ scheme and didn't now need me. I have also worked as a temporary ICT teacher in another local school, keeping a seat warm.

Recently, since then I have done nothing but supply teaching. I apply for every ICT job advertised, but only get interviewed about one time in twenty. I am well qualified in computers with an MSc, and over twenty years in the industry. Where do I go from here? In the absence of a real teaching job, do I walk away from the profession? I don't want to, but constant rejection does nothing for one's morale.

If the government spent just a fraction of the money they have put into schemes such as the former Fast Track scheme on offering career advice and counselling for people such as you, part of the teacher supply crisis would have disappeared a long while ago. However, that doesn't help you.

Sadly, although the open labour market for teachers has benefits, it also has drawbacks, as you have found. Completing training is no guarantee of a teaching job. The best schools have the pick of the trainees, and can choose the best quality at the lowest salary. Older teachers are often more expensive, and join staffrooms bulging with their contemporaries, when schools want younger teachers to balance the age profiles.

So what can you do? Perhaps check with someone who is prepared to be honest about your teaching skills. What do they see as your strengths and weaknesses in the classroom, and in your relations with those in authority? You may seem intimidating to others, without even realising you are. You are also trying to make a career at an age when others are looking to quit, and some heads may not believe you are in it for the long haul. Finding people who can give you advice is an urgent priority. Regrettably, there are few of them around to help people like you.

If you are free to move around, why not try the international schools circuit? Teachers in these schools often do only two or so years in a posting, and you could see something of the world while also teaching interesting classes. You should have sufficient experience to be attractive to these schools. Or have you considered further education as a possibility? It often doesn't pay as well as teaching in schools, but there can be other compensations, such as working with adults. Finally, can you talk with your supply agency to see if they can make better use of your talents, perhaps in finding you longer-term assignments?

The fact you have stuck at it for five years is to your credit. Sadly for you, the flow of newly qualified teachers of ICT is set to expand over the next few years. You will need to consider this fact in your future planning.

I had an interview with a supply agency recently. They asked me for a letter of application and my C.V. Having taught in Scotland for the past five years, I have never had to write such a letter. What should be included?

I would have thought that your C.V. would have been sufficient to demonstrate your teaching experience. I suppose that if they are going to interview you, then a letter of application provides a good starting point. The obvious point to address is, why do you want to become a supply teacher? The answer may simply be that your partner has relocated to a new part of the country and you want the opportunity to familiarise yourself with the area before opting for a permanent post. You might have other reasons such as mixing teaching and further study or family commitments, all of which would be perfectly appropriate. You can also use the letter to sell your C.V. by drawing attention to those points that merit attention and explaining anything that might seem a negative point.

How long will it take me to reach the top of the upper pay spine? I entered teaching this September.

The Main Scale now has six points (M1–M6). So, assuming you started at point 1, as almost everybody now does, you will reach point M6 at the start of your sixth year. If you then have the requisite two years' worth of necessary evidence and a Threshold Round is open, you may apply. Details of eligibility for the current round can be found at http://www.teachernet.gov.uk/management/payandperformance/performancethreshold/ on the DfES website.

Do you have to have been a teacher for any particular number of years before you can mentor an NQT for their induction year, and do you get any extra pay for mentoring?

Normally, you would expect to have been teaching for a few years before becoming a mentor. There is no point in offering help and guidance if you are not secure in your own teaching. However, sometimes either in small schools, or where there are few specialists, a less experienced teacher may be forced to take on the role as there is no one else available.

In these circumstances, if you are called on to be a mentor, you should ensure that you are offered training, and should also ask whether there is another member of staff to whom you can turn to for advice. As to whether you are likely to receive any extra pay for the role, much will depend upon whether you are provided with time for the role, or expected to add it to your existing duties. Mentoring of NQTs is not specifically mentioned in the Teachers' Pay and Conditions Document, but teachers can be required to contribute to 'the professional development of other teachers' so that may cover it. Different rules apply for the supervision of students on initial teacher training (ITT) courses.

I was employed in a school in London for three years, before moving abroad to teach in an international school. Last year, when I applied for a new post, the prospective employer was unable to obtain a reference from my first school. I learnt, eventually, that no reference was on file for me and that all the senior staff, including my former head of department, had left the school. The LEA has advised me that the school can only provides dates when I was employed, and that schools are not required to hold references on teachers. As you can imagine, my career may be severely impeded if I cannot provide a reference for three years of my professional life. What should I do?

It is often the case that not all your ideal referees may be available to you when you are seeking to change jobs. Clearly, your present employer can write of your current performance. It may be that you think you need a reference from someone in England to demonstrate your competence in teaching the National Curriculum. In that case, a reference from the institution where you trained might do just as well: presumably it helped get you the post in London in the first place. You can add a note to the application form explaining why you have not provided a reference from the London school. As your career progresses, this will cease to be an issue, as you will eventually have plenty of people you can call upon to act in this capacity.

I have been teaching in the same school without a break for twenty years. I arrived as a probationer and just never left. At first I taught 11-year-olds, but now I am a Reception class teacher. This year, for the first time, I am teaching the daughter of one of my original pupils, and it's a bit scary! I would like to take a term out for reflection and renewal. Can I ask my school for this length of time off?

Your question raises both personal and professional issues. Your employer has no need to grant any request you make for a term off, even without pay. However, as you are probably approaching the halfway point in your career, it would make sense for you to undertake a sustained period of professional development, and a good head would recognise this fact.

As an alternative, you could look for a new teaching post a term ahead, and create your own space. The best time to do this is during the autumn term, since, with the summer 'work break' added in, you can effectively create a five-month period away from the classroom. If you take this option, do remember to allow yourself time for re-entry. However, the most tax-efficient time for a short break can be from the half-term break in February until after half-term in May. This allows any loss of income to be offset across two tax years.

I have been teaching in the primary sector for my local education authority for 13 years. Wishing to take a short (three-month) career break, I resigned from my post at the end of December. During the break I completed my MA dissertation. I have now enrolled as a supply teacher but would like a full-time job again. I would appreciate your advice, particularly regarding the implications of my break from full-time employment for my teacher's pension and on tax-efficient timing.

Congratulations on gaining your MA degree. There should not be any long-term implications for your pension if you have a short break from teaching. You can rejoin the Teachers' Pension Scheme when you start full-time teaching again. Indeed, you should check with any supply agency you are registered with as to the possibility of making pension payments on your supply teaching income. You may also be able to 'buy in' the missing months for a small extra payment. Now you have your MA, you can apply for a wider range of posts. Although there are fewer posts in the primary sector than in the recent past, your experience and additional qualification should stand you in good stead.

I am an English as an Additional Language teacher, and I want to move to the countryside from inner London.

Your first step should be to check the job pages of the *TES* and websites such as *TES* online, at http://www.jobs.tes.co.uk, and *eteach,* at http://eteach.com. There are sections at the end of both the primary and the secondary job adverts that contain the sort of jobs you may be looking for; there may also be some posts advertised in the further education jobs section. One area you might consider is the education of Travellers' children. Many authorities have specific units working with such children and it might make an interesting new career challenge for someone with your background and experience.

I work as a tutor in the evenings to earn extra pay. Some of the parents of children in my school have found this out and want me to tutor their children. Would this be a good idea?

Many teachers take on extra part-time jobs. These include either working as tutors or marking examination papers. There is nothing wrong with this so long as it does not interfere with your full-time teaching post. As to tutoring children you teach, that is another matter. Generally, it is not advisable, because you could be faced with a conflict of interest. There is always the danger that a parent might feel you were not teaching their children properly, to ensure they came to you for extra paid tuition. You would be wiser to work only with children from outside of your school.

I was educated in an army school in Germany; do they still exist?

Yes, there are a few such schools left, mainly in Germany and Cyprus, but as the shape of Britain's armed forces alters, accompanied overseas postings are becoming rarer. If you want to work overseas, you should consider the much larger group of British schools overseas, where there is more chance to build a career. However, if you want a short period abroad, forces schools do still occasionally advertise posts in the *TES*.

As an NQT last year, I was paid on M1 (despite having past experience and a first degree). It was my own fault as I didn't push for a higher position on the pay scale. I read somewhere recently that if you have excellent performance in your first year you can ask to be moved up two points on the pay scale. Is this possible?

Technically, a school can add a discretionary point to the annual increment, 'where a teacher's performance in the previous school year was excellent with regard to all aspects of their professional duties, in particular classroom teaching'. That is what it says in the regulations. But trying to convince your head that you excel in everything as an NQT may be difficult, if not downright impossible. Your best opportunity would have been to have asked for more on the basis of your experience when you were appointed. Of course, the first degree isn't worth anything extra, as all teachers are expected to possess that level of qualification.

I am hoping you can give me some advice on changing jobs. I am considering moving to another job, but do not know how to approach it with my current school. I have seen a job advertised in the independent sector, and as I have always (eight years) worked in state schools I feel I could be seen as 'selling out'. If I do not get the job, then I am concerned that career prospects in my current school will be frozen. So, do I ask for testimonials from my head of department and head before applying? Do I discuss the fact that I am looking around for other jobs? What would you advise?

I always think it is better to be open with your employer. If you have given eight years' service, they cannot be surprised that you are looking to move on to further your career. However, you don't say how long you have been at this particular school. If you have a good relationship with the head, why not go and talk the issue of your career through, and ask for advice? If you don't get on, then you are going to leave anyway.

The job you want is in the independent sector. You might not be short-listed, so why tell the head any more than that you are looking for a new job? Your current head will always have to be a referee. Personally, I don't think testimonials are worth anything, as everyone knows that nobody says anything bad in an open document, even if the glowing tributes may make you feel better. It might be helpful if you could find someone from outside the school to act as a referee who could give a wider view on your abilities, such as a local authority officer or adviser or someone who has run a CPD activity you have taken part in recently.

I am currently a peripatetic drama teacher. I teach from nursery ages through to GCSE drama. Previously I have done two years at high school ages teaching drama at GCSE level. I am thinking of teaching in primary schools permanently in the future. How do I go about doing this, as my PGCE was for secondary drama teaching only?

Is there some kind of conversion course or would I have to go back to university?

Competition for teaching posts in the primary sector is tough at the moment: too many trained teachers and not enough jobs to go around. The fact that you have worked with primary-age children will be a help, but may not be enough by itself to allow you to make the change in career. Because of the oversupply, conversion courses don't really exist at this time. You actually don't need new certification, but attending some professional development courses for primary classroom teachers would be a sensible move. You might also talk with some of the primary head teachers you meet through your peripatetic work about the possibility of spending a week or so in their school on a voluntary basis. They might also advise you whether or not they can see you as a successful teacher in the primary sector. As a drama teacher, will you feel comfortable with, for instance, the numeracy curriculum, and the implications of seeing the same children week in and week out for a whole year? If you enjoy the peripatetic life, think seriously before making any change: the grass is not always greener on the other side.

I started as an NQT in my current school in September. I have found it difficult to settle into the area I now live in, as it is away from my parents and old friends. I am therefore considering moving back to the area where I used to live, if a new post becomes available for September. I was wondering how it would look to the school if I moved after one year, having completed my induction, and whether there would be any adverse reaction. I ask this as I will have to apply for jobs soon and will require time out for interviews. Any advice would be greatly appreciated.

There is an open market for teachers and anyone is free to test their worth at any time by applying for another post. The worst the school can say is that you have only been with it for one year. You need to reflect how easy it would be to find a job where you want to move back to. If it was a lack of jobs that caused you to move to your present post, consider how the school would feel if you said you were looking and then didn't find a post. It might affect the timetable they would be prepared to give you next year if they thought you would not be staying at the school. On the other hand, if your relations with your head of department are good, you might want to talk the issue through with them or with your mentor. It might be that this is just a case of mid-year 'blues' and what you need to do is focus on building roots in your new community.

I am an early career teacher, currently teaching a Reception class (although I consider myself a Key Stage 2 teacher). My degree is in politics and I've always liked the idea of using this in my teaching. I am considering making the jump to senior teaching and was interested to see positions advertised for secondary politics teachers. Would a head teacher ever consider someone like me for such a position? (I have taught in KS2 and have previous experience of working with teenagers.) If not, how can I gain the necessary skills to enable me to make the jump?

Posts to teach politics are rare in the schools sector, although they may be more common in the FE sector. A better route might be to look for a school that is seeking general class teachers to teach a range of subjects to pupils new to the secondary sector. These schools often welcome teachers with experience of the primary sector. If you find such a school, you might also be able to negotiate some specialist teaching as well. Apart from these options, you may find that heads will always try to appoint secondary-trained teachers. With more teachers being trained than in recent years, making the switch between sectors is likely to prove ever more difficult. There are, however, some posts teaching social studies, and even humanities, that you might also consider. But as the table in Appendix A shows, even these are relatively few and far between at both the classroom teacher and head of department levels.

I work as a part-time NQT. I started my induction year on 1 November on a 0.7 contract. This was increased in the following September to 0.8. I am still on M1 spinal point and wonder whether I should have progressed to M2 in the following September or should expect to have an increase in salary at the end of my induction in February? Or will I have to wait until next September to move up to M2?

The pay level of classroom teachers has to be determined from 1 September each year. Normally, if you are not on the maximum of the main scale, you should receive an increment. However, there are certain circumstances in which the head can advise governing bodies not to pay the increment, but you must be told and should have a right to appeal. If the head has not told you of any reason why you did not receive an increment, then I suggest you ask your professional association to investigate what has happened.

I am a secondary-trained NQT, teaching French and Spanish. I have twelve years' experience of teaching EFL [English as a foreign language] to both adults and children (aged 3 years and up). As an EFL teacher I held positions of responsibility for young learner sections of various schools. Before leaving France to do my PGCE, I worked as a peripatetic teacher of English in four primary schools. I would very much like to be involved in teaching MFL [Modern foreign languages] in primary schools in Britain (either delivering classes or training teachers), but am not sure how to break into the sector. Do you have any advice or suggestions? My secondary school does not have language college status, and I do not have any formal training as a teacher trainer, although I have led and developed CPD sessions in various schools in various countries.

There may well be two possible routes, but neither will be easy. You could try to move into the primary sector in a school with a languages programme and gain some expertise that way. Alternatively, you need to look for posts working with the primary sector helping to train teachers. One way to become known would be to register for a part-time higher degree researching into some aspect of foreign language teaching in the primary sector. This would allow you to develop some contacts and you could combine your study with teaching. You could, of course, also look for a post in a school with language college status that undertakes out-reach work with the primary sector. All these options may require you to be flexible and move to where the jobs are. If that is a problem, you may need to research what might be available in your local area.

I have just been given the responsibility for teaching gymnastics to KS1 and KS2. I am a fully qualified teacher with a background in gymnastics and am looking for a one- or two-day course that includes health and safety, before September.

You are sensible to want to be as well informed about health and safety as possible. Your first port of call should be a web search. I turned up a number of websites with a search of 'PE and Health & Safety'. No doubt the addition of 'gymnastics' or 'primary' would further refine the search and tailor it more to your needs. It seems that there is a lot of advice out there. Many local authorities have also produced policy documents to cover health and safety, and these can be found on the web as well. You might then want to check your school's policy against these, to see if it needs updating. However, there is a risk that you might be given responsibility for your school's general health and safety policy, and not just for gymnastics, if you show too much interest. It is questionable whether such a responsibility would qualify for Teaching and Learning Responsibility (TLR) payments under the new system, especially if part of the responsibility was for areas not related to teaching and learning.

I am currently in my fifth year of teaching and have resigned from my current post. I have been for six interviews despite being a teacher in a shortage subject. The jobs I have gone for keep going to NQTs. I am worried that there may be few jobs left for September. I have never had any problem getting a job before and the feedback I have been given has all been very vague and conflicting. Do you have any advice?

Many teachers make the mistake of believing that because there were serious teacher recruitment problems a few years ago, there will always be a job when they want one. A combination of increased output from teacher training courses in all subjects and the early stages of a long-term decline in the secondary school population means that the boom time for teachers wanting to shift posts may soon be a thing of the past, as many primary school teachers and trainees are finding out. Fewer pupils means smaller budgets for schools, despite headline increases in overall budgets. In the secondary sector, NQTs are still cheaper to employ than more experienced teachers, even with the extra non-teaching time for the Induction Year. It may be that you will need to explain to schools why you are changing posts so often. Some heads may consider you are not a good longer-term investment, and therefore opt for someone younger and less well qualified. Even though you have been receiving different types of feedback, a process that is notoriously random in nature, are there any common themes in what has been said? Finally, you are gaining interviews, so is it something that happens on the day that is letting you down, or is it just that shortages are now a thing of the past?

I am in serious need of another job so I can work out my notice. I teach in the private sector, and have been in the same school since I qualified as a mature entrant two years ago. I have a joint degree and want to change subject without stepping back down the career ladder. I am currently head of subject at my school and I enjoy curriculum planning, teaching and pastoral work, but have never taught my second subject. How should I go about finding another job?

You don't say why you need another job and want to leave. I think you are asking a lot to expect to find a management job in a subject you have never taught. Why do you want to change both subject and school at the same time? It would be easier just to keep to the subject you know best and look for another post in that subject. Also, if you are not offered what you want, you may have to decide whether to take a post at a lower salary and work your way back up to head of department or hold out for the management post. Much will depend upon the job market in the area where you are looking and the skills you have to offer. As a mature entrant, you may have additional skills that are of interest to a school, along with your subject expertise.

2 Life beyond the Main Scale

With the Main Scale now having only six points, teachers quickly reach the point at which they become eligible to cross the threshold. At such a major point, this is an important time to review your longer-term goals and to check on your career path. What options are still open to you, and what routes are either now closed or more difficult to follow? There are many different career options: progress through the three points of the upper pay spine, look for an opening either as an Advanced Skills Teacher or on the Excellent Teacher Scheme, or a move on to the Leadership Scale as either an assistant head or deputy head.

Since the start of 2006, schools have only been able to reward teachers for extra responsibilities associated with teaching and learning (Teaching and Learning Responsibility points). There are two grades, known as TLR2 and TLR1, with the latter having the greater payments attached to it. Although the government has not prescribed set figures for salaries within these two bands, unofficial intermediate rates have been developed by schools and are becoming generally accepted within the marketplace.

The staffing review that preceded the introduction of the TLR points allowed some schools to totally rethink their staffing structures, and a number of new job titles such as 'Leaders of Learning' for particular year or age groups emerged to replace the former pastoral system.

I have been teaching for six years and, although I still enjoy what I am doing, I wonder whether it is time to look for more responsibility.

This has to be a personal decision. At this point in time you should have some idea of where you see your life going for at least the next few years. Beyond the near horizon you may have more vaguely defined aspirations and, perhaps, an eventual career goal. If you haven't really thought of the need to take charge of your career, now is the time to take stock. If you came into teaching after a career doing something else, you will probably appreciate the need for keeping your prospects under review. However, if you trained immediately after finishing your degree, you may not have thought about the longer-term picture in any detail.

Now is the time to focus on those questions about what you want from your life and your career. If you enjoy what you are doing, why are you questioning whether you should make any changes? Maybe you recognise that, although the work is still fulfilling, and always will be, there might be more to life than just classroom teaching. You will need to consider what steps you should take to prepare yourself for your next move. Assuming that at this stage you want to remain within a school setting, there are two main avenues open to you: either take responsibility for the work of others or change direction.

Taking responsibility for others involves possibly the biggest change you will experience during your career in teaching. For the first time you will have direct responsibility for the work of other adults as a line manager. Of course, this is easier for many teachers now than it used to be, as classrooms are no longer self-contained boxes where teachers work in isolation from each other. If you are working within an early years setting, you will have been used to leading a team of other professionals from the day you started in the classroom. Many teachers in the primary and special school sectors have also been used to setting work for support staff and liaising with other helpers. However, for many secondary teachers, although working with other staff is becoming more common than in the past, taking responsibility for the work of others is still not the norm.

Of course, there are some areas of the secondary curriculum where schools often have only one specialist and rely upon the use of either part-time staff or even less well qualified teachers to ensure that the timetable is fully staffed. Such teachers, in subjects such as music and RE, will often have had to take responsibility from day one of their careers.

Nevertheless, whether this is an area where you have been learning 'on the job', or one where you are looking to take responsibility for the first time, you should seek out some professional training. Staff responsibility is a much more complicated area than it was in the past. Not for nothing have personnel departments transformed themselves into human resources units. Their new name more clearly spells out the role that those responsible for other staff now have within an organisation.

If you don't want to take responsibility for the work of others at this point in your career, you can look at the other main alternative; developing some other skill or competence.

For some this might mean a switch in age groups. At present, all teachers in England have the same qualification, although they will have been through many different training routes. However, switching between phases is more difficult than it used to be. With falling rolls in the primary sector likely to persist throughout the first decade of this century, and healthy intakes into training courses for primary-sector teachers, switching from subject-based secondary teaching to the more class-based environment of many primary schools isn't as easy as many teachers would wish. A secondary school teacher wishing to switch to the primary sector, or indeed a junior-trained teacher wanting to teach Reception-age children, might find their existing experience of little value when applying for such posts. At the present time there is little on offer by way of conversion courses for anyone wanting to make this type of move.

So how can it be achieved? Assuming you feel confident in being able to teach the whole range of curriculum areas you will face, there is still the matter of how to deliver that curriculum appropriately for the age group and how to monitor and assess their individual needs. One possibility is to look for part-time or distance learning courses offered by academic institutions. Another way is to offer to act in a liaison role between your school and the groups you are seeking to teach. This may also help you clarify why you want to make such a move. But in the present climate it won't be easy.

Much easier is looking for professional development that will allow you to move into another area of responsibility within your present school. Two obvious areas are special needs and information technology. Most schools have co-ordinator roles in these areas, and few teachers will have been trained for such roles. These are both areas where an interest can be a first starting point and lead you to search out professional development courses that specifically prepare you for a school-wide co-ordination role.

Is it better to go on lots of different courses or gain a further academic qualification before looking for promotion?

Until fairly recently the answer would have been easy: enrol on a higher degree course. However, with the development of the concept of individual 'portfolios' that can be built up over a period of time, there is now a range of acceptable alternatives. Nevertheless, there is little point is amassing a random collection of professional development activities that have no coherence to them. Try to focus on programmes that are of use either in your current job or for the next one you are aiming at.

Academic qualifications do have the advantage that they are assessed and, as a result, someone will be able to provide an objective view of your involvement with the material. Most other activities will merely be able to provide a certificate of attendance, which will confirm only that you were present.

I have been teaching in the same secondary school for the past five years since I finished my training. Although I am a hard-working teacher, and the department had a successful Ofsted report some years ago, soon after I started at the school I began to feel that my career is being blocked. My head of department is close to the head teacher and suggests that I will not be promoted within the school, but should move elsewhere. Thus, I am concerned that I might not receive a fair reference were I to move on. Is there anything I can do about the discrimination I feel is being directed towards me?

There are a number of important points raised by your question. What is a sensible length of time to spend in your first teaching post? After five years you will have seen almost a whole cohort pass through the main part of the school. Therefore, in career terms this might be a sensible time to look for another post, if your aim is to develop a career. Your head of department might actually be doing you a favour. You also write of your career 'being blocked' within the school. Unless you have some hard evidence, such as repeatedly being rejected for internal posts you have applied for and unsatisfactory reasons being given in any debriefings, this would be a difficult matter to prove. There have to have been opportunities for promotion within the school that were open to you. In teaching, you are responsible for your own career, so your head of department or head teacher has no specific duty to look after your career progression, although you should expect help with career development.

Unless there is some particular malice towards you, I can't see why you think you would receive a bad reference if you applied for another teaching post. These days, it is usually possible to see what others have written about you, and to challenge any blatant untruths. However, if you are worried, it is sensible to look for a possible referee from outside the school such as a local adviser or someone who has organised professional development courses you have taken part in recently. Such a person might also be prepared to give you some unbiased advice about both your professional skills and how you present yourself.

If, in the end, you think it is more than just a clash of personalities, and you feel that you have some concrete evidence of discrimination, then you should talk with your professional association. Perhaps it would be better to contact the branch secretary rather than your school representative if you feel that the latter is too close to the situation you find confronting you.

I am thinking of changing my job, but I have been in my current post since I was an NQT. How do I write a letter of application selling myself? Are there any guidelines to follow?

This is a tough question as you don't give away much information. I don't know how long you have been teaching and in what type of school, and what sort of post you are looking for.

Try to draw up a balance sheet of what you want from your new job and what you can offer any school. Continuity is obviously something you can offer; you won't be off next year to another post. Some schools like that, others like turnover. Why have you stayed put? I spent seven years in one school early in my career just to work with a whole cohort from form teacher when they arrived, to a couple doing A levels in my subject. Very satisfying, but then I felt it was time to move on.

I am in my second year of teaching and was appointed the unpaid ICT co-ordinator after completing my NQT year in a large primary school. Is this post eligible for TLR payments?

The answer will depend upon how your school carried out its staffing review in the autumn of 2005. There is nothing to prevent you, as a second-year teacher, from receiving a TLR supplement for an appropriate post. If you are responsible for co-ordinating the work of other teachers, then you would seem to have a strong case. But the problem may be how much co-ordination you are required to do. Preparing teaching materials and even the odd training session almost certainly won't be enough to qualify. Much may depend upon the state of the school budget.

I am confused about some of the adverts for TLRs. They seem to imply that there are points such as 2a or 1c within both TLR1 and TLR2. What do they mean?

When any change occurs, such as the introduction of TLRs, there may be a period of confusion. There are no 'official' salary points within the two TLR salary bands as contained within the official Teachers' Pay and Conditions document. However, as any two teachers on the same TLR, but at different salaries, must be separated by a £1,500 differential, some unofficial systems have emerged based upon steps calculated up from the bottom of the two TLR ranges. It is too early to tell whether they will become common currency. At present they may only serve to confuse many people, not just you.

Can I be asked to co-ordinate a subject without a TLR allowance?

It all depends upon what is meant by co-ordination. In a small primary school, where all teachers co-ordinate different parts of the curriculum on an equal basis, the budget probably won't stretch, even though there is a case for everyone to have a payment. Indeed, the level of coordination would probably fall within the responsibilities expected of any class-room teacher. In a secondary school, where there are defined areas of responsibility, then co-ordination is a formal responsibility and should not be undertaken unless you are being paid for the responsibility, particularly if you are responsible for the work of other staff members.

At present I have a post in a large primary school with responsibility for literacy at Key Stage 1. After some years doing this work I would like some more general responsibilities. Should I start applying for assistant head teacher posts or ignore them and move straight on to deputy headships?

This is a difficult question to answer. From the tone of your question, you are looking to find a foothold on the leadership ladder with the possible eventual chance of becoming a head teacher. As primary schools range in size from those with over 600 pupils to small schools with fewer than 100 pupils, your first decision concerns the type of school you want to work in. Your present post is in a large primary school and it may be that this kind of school is where you would feel most comfortable. Some of these schools are now advertising assistant headships, but they are still relatively rare, except in London and the South East. Most small schools can't afford to have both an assistant head and a deputy as well as the head teacher. So if you want to work in a small school, you will have to apply for a deputy headship anyway. Overall, there seems little to be gained from applying for an assistant headship in your case.

I am in my third year of teaching and have been acting head of department since September, when my head of department went on maternity leave. I am applying for a head of department post elsewhere. Any advice on the kind of things to put into an application letter? Also, I am a bit concerned about my experience. After only three years in the job, is this really enough to become a head of department?

In any letter of application you are trying to answer two questions: can you do the job and why do you want it? Start by looking at the person and job specifications. Then try to match up your experience with what is required. The better the fit, the more chance you stand of being interviewed and even being offered the post. However, some jobs attract far more applications than others, and this will affect who is selected for interview. As to whether three years is sufficient experience, ask yourself whether others will have more and better experience and why you want the job now. Have you enjoyed your period as an acting head of department and, if so, why? Some schools may regard three years as insufficient and others as showing keenness. You will have to address the issue either in the application or at interview, so think your answer through.

I am in my third year of teaching ICT and desperately want to work overseas for a while. How do I find out more about schools in different countries? I take it that most of them do not have Ofsted? Can I rely on the information published in brochures and on websites?

Each country regulates its schools in its own way. If you want to teach in an international school, you can check whether it is accredited or not. This will tell you something about the way the school operates. Otherwise, you could ask the teachers' professional bodies in the countries you want to teach in; but be prepared for a lack of information in some countries.

You could resort to the internet and either post a question on a bulletin board or enter a chatroom discussion, but you will find it hard to check the validity of the information you receive. Finally, you could always work abroad through one of the exchange schemes that will undertake to find the placement for you. Check out the British Council website at http://www.britishcouncil.org./learning-ie-teaching-exchange.htm for some details. There are also other programmes such as the VIF Scheme. Their advertisements are in the jobs pages of the *TES*. Spending time abroad in this way can be a valuable experience.

I am in my sixth year of primary teaching and I have taught in Years 1 to 3. However, I have been considering changing to secondary for some time. I would love to teach English language and Literature. I have a four-year B.Ed. degree and specialised in history and English. Would I also have to do an MA in English in order to teach to secondary level?

Your qualified teacher status (QTS) is officially enough to allow you to transfer, so you could just go ahead and apply for posts you see advertised in the *TES*. However, you need to ask yourself what sort of timetable you would like; and whether your B.Ed. contains sufficient subject knowledge to stretch able pupils. The QTS standards emphasise development of subject knowledge, so an MA might seem a good idea, but you need to ensure it is relevant to the secondary curriculum. Without it, you might find yourself with a restricted timetable and employed just because you were good with the younger pupils. It is worth talking to a local English adviser or head of department in a secondary school to get their perspective on your qualifications.

I am an English teacher in a secondary school with three years' experience. I want to stay in education in some capacity, but am desperate to get out of the hectic, pressurised daily life in school. Because of family commitments, I can't move from the rural area where I live. I need to earn a reasonable amount each month to make ends meet, but I am not ambitious. Can you give me some ideas as to what I might do?

Letters like yours are all too common at this time of year. Having made sure it is not just the mid-year blues, you should ask yourself what it was that attracted you to teaching in the first place. In addition, check with your friends outside teaching whether they feel their own jobs are 'hectic and pressurised'. It seems that such descriptions are not restricted to teachers these days. However, if the life is getting too much for you, and it is not anything the school can do something about, you are right to evaluate possible alternative careers.

If you are determined to look elsewhere, what alternatives are there? You could consider switching into education administration. Most education officers started their careers as teachers. Alternatively, you could take a course to tutor students in English as a foreign language. This can cover everything from working with teenagers to helping executives become proficient in English. It might also be possible to combine this work with earning extra money by offering accommodation as well as teaching. Other possibilities include looking to the private sector for a post as a training officer, or offering to teach adult education classes. However, this might include some evening work and might also mean working for several different colleges. Finally, you can always decide to work for yourself.

When I was young, I spent some time in hospital where a teacher attached to the hospital taught me. Do such posts still exist and how would I go about finding one?

These days, fewer children spend long periods in hospital than in the past, often as a result of changes in medical care. However, there are still a small number of hospital schools and units around Britain that are staffed by professional teachers. In total, there are probably fewer than 100 posts in such schools, so they are hard to come by. Those posts that there are appear in the jobs pages and require a degree of versatility, since there is little room for subject specialist work. As an alternative, have you considered working with children who are being educated at home for whatever reason? Most local authorities provide this service for a number of their pupils, and jobs may be easier to come by.

I've been teaching for over ten years, and decided it would be useful to use the 360-degree evaluation technique for a critical reflection of my own teaching alongside a SWOT analysis. I waited until the planning and school reports were out of the way before producing my own modified version of the evaluation. It was modified so that the questions and criteria fitted onto a single sheet of paper with space for comments on the back. Instructions were given orally.

I asked my head and deputy on a Monday if they would mind filling one out for me and giving it back to me by the Friday. I was met with indifference, and then concern about my overloading some NQTs with extra work after the head discovered I had asked one of them as well. What should I do?

I can understand your frustrations; 360-degree appraisal can be a very powerful tool. It may be that your head doesn't fully understand what you were trying to do. That said, is this just an isolated breakdown in communications, or is it a symptom of a deeper-seated problem? Without knowing more about the background, it is difficult to advise you; but could your head feel threatened? You have been teaching for ten years, but don't say how long you have been at the school. Have you been there longer than the head? Is it time to move on, perhaps to a post with more responsibility?

My head of department is soon to begin maternity leave and I have been informally asked to take over the running of the department in her absence. I am keen to take on a role that will aid my career development (some practical experience to put on my CV would be useful), but I don't want to be seen as someone who works for nothing.

And so you shouldn't. The days of doing something for nothing in teaching should now be long gone. The government has effectively been changing and clarifying the rules over the past few years. If you are required to undertake work in a leadership role, then you must be paid for that work, even if it is the lowest amount on the new TLR2 scale. As this is a maternity leave cover, you should expect to be offered a temporary payment covering the maternity leave. If the job entails the same work, then you should be paid the same amount as the substantive head of department. Make sure that it is all documented and above board, don't do anything unofficially.

What has happened to the Advanced Skills Teacher grade? I don't see many posts advertised for ASTs in English. Has the grade disappeared in one of the revamps to the pay scales?

No, the grade is still in existence. It was created about a decade ago in order to offer an alternative route to promotion for teachers who didn't want to go down the management route and become a head of department. The AST grade made a slow start, partly because of government demands about ASTs needing to have a wider role that included work with other schools. There were also complications over funding the posts. Although these issues have disappeared, ASTs never really seem to have caught the imagination of the teaching profession. Most nationally advertised AST posts are concentrated in shortage subjects such as mathematics and ICT. Of course, schools may be appointing such teachers, but not advertising nationally; that would not help your quest to find such a post.

3 Looking for leadership

At some point in their careers, many teachers find themselves with responsibilities for other adults. Around one in eight teachers who enter the primary sector have ended up as either head teachers or deputies; it is certain many did not start out with that aim in mind. Although the percentage of teachers who become heads or deputies in the secondary sector is lower, many teachers acquire additional responsibilities, often as part of a middle tier of leadership. For some, this is as far as they will want to go. Teaching will remain the focus of their professional life, and the 'politics' associated with responsibility, let alone the bureaucracy, holds little interest. For others, this first step on the leadership ladder will be the start of a new phase in their careers that will offer a whole new range of opportunities.

Is it better to become an Advanced Skills Teacher or an assistant head teacher? I am currently second in a mathematics department and considering my options for the future.

To answer this question I really need to know where you see your career in teaching going in the longer term. Although the Advanced Skills Teacher (AST) grade was designed to offer a career structure for teachers who wanted to stay in touch with the classroom, it doesn't really seem to have taken off. At one point the government was talking of 5,000 such teachers. Part of the problem may be in the way entry to the grade is handled.

On the other hand, the assistant head grade can be used by schools however they see fit. Although it frequently takes teachers out of the classroom for part of the week by adding leadership tasks, some schools are now being more creative. Adverts have been appearing that allow curriculum specialists in areas like maths, English and ICT to assume a whole-school role for the development of their subject while retaining a substantial amount of teaching. Assuming you may be looking for further promotion in the future, this could be an interesting option. Why not see if there is someone in your local authority you can speak to on possible career development issues and your options? Nevertheless, since the staffing review there has been a slight upturn in adverts for ASTs. Whether this will continue after the 'excellent teacher' grade is introduced, only time will tell, but I have my doubts.

Do I need to have completed the National Professional Qualification for Headship before I apply for my first headship?

Since 1 April 2004 it has been mandatory for all first-time head teachers in the maintained sector in England to hold the NPQH or to have secured a place on the programme that leads to the qualification. The position is different in Wales, and anyone wanting to apply for a headship in Wales should check the latest position there. The NPQH is a programme focused on an individual's training and development requirements. The amount of time needed for the programme depends on a person's existing qualifications, experience, skills and expertise. Anyone very close to being ready for headship may be able to progress to the final stage of NPQH in as little as four months. However, according to the National College, the expectation is that candidates will take a maximum of two years to complete the NPQH and then be ready to apply for a headship.

In May 2003 the National College reported that there were nearly 7,000 people working towards the NPQH, and more than 8,000 have graduated with the qualification since its introduction in 1997. However, figures for completion and success rates do not seem to be available. It is now possible to accredit the NPQH towards a higher degree at a number of universities. You may be interested to know that around 10 per cent of schools advertise for a new head teacher each year.

How likely am I to need to move to find a headship? I have three children at sensitive stages of their education and I don't want to disturb them at this time.

Much will depend upon what sort of school you are looking to become the head of. Each year, between 2,000 and 2,500 schools of all types advertise for a new head teacher. About 25 per cent of appointments go to existing heads who are changing schools. The remainder are mostly filled by deputy heads who are becoming a head teacher for the first time. It seems that the average length of time a head spends in post these days is probably slightly less than ten years – longer in pleasant suburban and rural areas, but shorter in challenging inner-city schools.

From your local knowledge, you should be able to calculate how many vacancies are likely to occur within reasonable travelling distance of where you live during the next couple of years. However, if you are looking for a particular type of school, either a specialist secondary school or, perhaps, a church primary school, you may need to cast your net a little wider.

I am a deputy head in an independent school. I have been looking into applying for the NPQH but my school will not finance me, on the reasonable assumption that, after gaining the qualification, I will gain a headship and leave the school. Is there any other source of funding, or will I have to pay the £3,000 myself?

Sadly, I think you will have to pay. However, your head may be short-sighted in not offering any help. Schools that promote good staff development policies can usually attract more applicants. This makes sound business sense and is good for retention, as it improves morale. However, heads do have to balance the cost against the potential benefit to both the school and yourself.

My primary school is thinking of advertising for an assistant head teacher. What are the advantages of this post?

The grade of assistant head teacher was introduced a few years ago. It offers a useful first step on the leadership ladder for teachers. As the decision to employ an assistant head is one for the school, it seems to have proved a more flexible change than the introduction of the Advanced Skills Teacher grade some years earlier. The advantage to your school will depend partly upon its size. Small primary schools that can't afford a deputy head post may find that an assistant head offers an alternative way to recruit someone for the head to share the leadership of the school with. For larger schools, it offers a route to develop new leadership structure that can be flexible in nature, since many assistant heads can be expected to progress to deputy head posts after a few years.

I recently saw a post of head of religious education advertised on the assistant head teacher grade. Can a school actually do this?

So long as the job has a school-wide function, and is concerned with leadership, there would seem to be no reason why such a post could not be created. Some schools have been advertising for heads of either numeracy or literacy at assistant head teacher level for some time, and there have also been adverts for leadership in IT across the school. There are factors associated with transferring on to the leadership grade that needs to be considered, such as the changes in conditions of service compared with serving on the Main Scale. The most important of these may be the loss of defined working time and all that implies. Any potential applicant would need to check the salary benefits against the changes in terms and conditions that would arise from no longer being on the Main Scale for teachers. This also applies to those becoming ASTs. You are no longer covered by the directed time and maximum working days limits.

I have an interview for a deputy head post. What questions are likely to come up? It is a primary school, by the way. If you could give me some examples of the types of questions I am likely to face, that would be marvellous.

There are a number of obvious areas, such as your teaching expertise, leadership and management experience and relationships with the many different groups of adults that it's the head's lot to come across. The balance of questions may differ depending upon the size of the school, and its location. Will you be a full-time classroom teacher with a bit of time off for the deputy role, or is it a large school with a significant amount of non-teaching time? If the post carries responsibility for a particular age phase, such as under-fives or for the extended school day, you must expect questions about the leadership of those activities. Some questions may be couched in general terms, such as what current policies will have the most impact on primary schools over the next five years; or they may be quite specific. There are plenty of all-purpose books on how to succeed at interview, and a search of the *TES* website will reveal some more specific advice from those who have already been there. Remember, the head will once have been sitting where you are, and should understand how you feel. But do expect to be rigorously tested on both your knowledge and your opinions.

I have been teaching for five years, always the same year group. I have vast experience with SATs and am a mentor to both trainees and NQTs, and I have the role of assessment co-ordinator and team leader for a key stage. What can I do next? I am still in my late twenties, but would like to go the deputy head route. I would rather not move school, but I am willing to go to develop my career. What would you advise?

There are going to be lots of leadership posts available in the next few years, as many primary heads and deputies retire. Many deputies in primary schools were under 35 when appointed last year. However, according to DfES figures, only a handful of deputies were under 30. You might consider both widening your experience through taking a different year group, and enrolling on a programme of professional development, perhaps one leading to a higher degree. This will both widen your experience and increase your professional understanding. If you have spent your entire career in the same school, you might well want to move schools. This would be both a challenge and an opportunity to work in another setting. Only about one in four schools appoint an internal candidate to a deputy headship, and when they do, it is often because they have no alternative.

I am currently looking for deputy head posts and was wondering how the Leadership Scale worked. Should I just be looking at L1 posts, or am I able to jump on to the Leadership Scale at, say, L4?

Each school decides the appropriate salary range for the post it is advertising. The range for a deputy is normally five points on the Leadership Scale. For reasons that date well back into history, the larger the school, the higher the range. This means that small primary schools pay less than large secondary schools for jobs with the same title. I have always wondered whether this is entirely fair. Schools can increase the range offered where there are likely to be recruitment difficulties. These days, that means almost anywhere in the country. You can, therefore, apply for a post starting at any point on the Leadership Scale and, where a range is specified in the advert, you can negotiate to start above the bottom of the range. However, that will mean the possibility of fewer increments in years to come.

I have recently taken on the post of head of PE on a TLR2 as part of a creative arts faculty, led by a faculty manager. Over a two-week period (fifty one-hour lessons) I have five PPA [planning, preparation and assessment] periods and three free periods (unprotected from cover). Is this adequate time for the position I hold?

If your school is operating a ten-day timetable, then I guess the five lessons is equal to 10 per cent, over the ten days. Even though the actual wording refers to a week, I think it would be accepted that in this case it means a timetable cycle of ten days.

As to whether the three other lessons are adequate, what does everyone else in a similar position receive? Admin work should now be done by people other than teachers, which should include any lists you prepare for teams and booking fixtures and transport. If other heads of departments have more non-contact time, your first move would be to ask why you receive less. If there is no sensible answer, I would think that you should then ask why you do not receive the same amount as others on the same grade.

4 Alternative career routes

A teaching qualification can be a passport to many other jobs. There are those associated with education, but beyond the normal classroom experience, such as working with children and young people with special or individual needs. There are also many other posts that are ancillary to schools, whether in educational administration, publishing, museums, field centres, inspection, or in training the next generation of teachers and classroom assistants. Some of these alternative posts can provide a new career path with opportunities for promotion; others allow the development of particular interests, but do not provide a career structure.

I want to work with children with special educational needs. How do I go about retraining?

There are many different types of special needs. Some can be catered for within mainstream schools, but others still need separate schools, occasionally within a residential setting. Staffing these 'special' schools with trained professionals is often a somewhat haphazard affair. Much like initial teacher training, you can either undertake a course of professional training before looking for a teaching post or you can apply for a post and train part-time while working. As budgets have been devolved down to schools, the funds for full-time training courses have often disappeared. This has caused some courses to fold through a lack of applicants.

I have been offered a post with a company supplying the education market. They have a pension plan but, in view of all the publicity about pensions, I don't know what to do with my contributions to the Teachers' Pension Scheme.

Advice about pensions can be technical and is best obtained from an expert, who can assess your individual circumstances. However, there are some questions you would certainly want to ask. First, what sort of scheme does the company run? Is it a final salary scheme, like the Teachers' Pension Scheme, or is it what is called a 'money purchase scheme'? In a money purchase scheme, your contributions are used to provide a cash sum to purchase an annuity on retirement. Second, what is the history of the scheme? Is it regarded as 'fully funded' at present, and what level of contributions does the employer make to the fund? What would your contributions be? Finally, what are the various benefits available, including any continuation of the pension after your death for a partner, death in service grants, as well as the level of any lump sum payment? With all this information, you can decide to ask how the scheme compares to the other options available to you. Do remember that if there is a chance that you might return to the education sector at some time in the future, you will need to take that into account as well.

Where can I find information about training to become an educational psychologist?

Educational psychologists are concerned with children's learning and development, working primarily in schools with teachers and parents. They carry out a wide range of tasks with the aim of enhancing children's learning and enabling teachers to become more aware of the social factors affecting teaching and learning.

At present, the qualifications and training to become Registered as a Chartered Educational Psychologist in England, Wales and Northern Ireland, mean it is normally necessary to complete the following:

- an appropriate accredited qualification in psychology (1–4 years) to obtain the Graduate Basis for Registration;
- a teaching qualification (i.e. PGCE, a PGCE Conversion or B.Ed) (1–3 years);
- teaching experience with children and young adults up to the age of 19 years (2 years);
- an accredited postgraduate training course in educational psychology (1 year);
- supervised experience as an educational psychologist (1 year).

The initial training route for educational psychologists has been under review by a DfES facilitated working group. The British Psychological Society has approved of changes supporting a training route that will no longer require teacher training and teaching experience. It would consist of GBR plus three years' postgraduate training based in part at a university and in part on placements relevant to the work of an Educational Psychologist.

The implementation date will depend on the outcome of a DfES spending bid to fund the new training model. According to the British Psychological Society web site the DfES announced in November 2003 that 'there can be no guarantee that funding will be found to enable implementation in the original planned start year of 2005'. For more information here is the link to the appropriate part of the BPS web site. www.bps.org.uk/careers/careers3.cfm#educational.

I have been teaching history for some years but am fed up with all the clerical work. However, I still enjoy teaching my subject. Are there any other career possibilities you can suggest?

These days there are a number of opportunities outside of the classroom that someone in your position can consider. The growth in the heritage industry in recent years has been accompanied by the creation of many education officer posts working at specific locations ranging from pre-historic sites to re-creations of Victorian villages. Many of these reflect the industrial and social heritage of the country and require a degree of interest and enthusiasm for the period. There are also posts attached to the more conventional museums; these may have a range of different galleries, although there may also be a specific focus.

The advantage of working with a whole range of different pupils, whom you will often see only for a very short period of time, has to be balanced by the loss of any chance to see a group of pupils develop their knowledge and understanding in your subject.

Finally, I am puzzled about your reference to 'clerical work'. Are you still doing tasks outlawed under the Workload Agreement? I know that as the signing of the agreement slips into history, it is possible for some teachers to forget what it covered. Perhaps you need a copy displayed prominently in your staffroom?

How do I find a post in television working on education programmes?

Such jobs are relatively rare, and competition is often fierce for those that do arise. Sometimes they are advertised in the education press, but more often they are to be found among other advertisements for posts in the media. You will need a first-class knowledge of your subject area and will also need to be able to demonstrate some experience of curriculum development and the use of the media in delivering the curriculum. It will help to have some understanding of how television works, but it is unlikely that you will be required to be an expert. Sometimes people take any position available to 'get a foot in the door'. There is a risk attached to this method as there is no guarantee that your teaching skills will be up to date when the ideal post is advertised.

**I have seen a post as an advisory teacher advertised. It
sounds good but they didn't say what the holidays were. I
don't want to ring them up and ask in case it looks as if
that's all I'm interested in about the post. Do these posts
normally have the same holidays as teachers, since they
involve working in schools?**

Generally, posts that are outside schools may be paid either under the
Teachers' Pay and Conditions Document or under local government conditions of service. You should ask whether there is any local agreement.
Apart from the difference in holidays, another point to watch is the pension arrangements. Some posts under local government conditions may
not be linked into the Teachers' Pension Scheme. It may not matter at this
point in time, but it is always worth checking both the contribution levels
paid by the employee and the employer and whether the benefits are the
same. However, in the end it is whether the job is what you want that will
probably matter most.

How do I become an HMI as opposed to an 'Inspector'?

The post of Her Majesty's Inspector of Schools has a long and hon-
ourable history going back to the start of state-funded education in
England over 150 years ago. Most of those who inspect schools these
days are just 'Inspectors' appointed with a limited brief to conduct
inspections. However, some HMIs, as they are more commonly known,
are still appointed following adverts in the national and educational
press such as the *TES*. HMIs are usually experts in particular fields of
education and teaching but can be called upon to undertake a wider
range of work than inspections. The system in Wales is slightly different
from that in England.

I have been teaching for a number of years and wonder what is the career path to becoming a Director of Education or a Chief Education Officer.

Although schools have more control over their affairs than in the past, all local authorities still have an education service of some sort that requires leadership from professional officers. Most are former teachers who have made the career move into governance and administration at some point in their careers. The usual route is to start with a lower-level post and progress through the ranks. However, it is possible to transfer later to a more senior post if you have some additional skills. Some areas require a degree of specialist knowledge, such as leading the centrally based special needs teams that often include Pupil Referral Units and have overall responsibility for special needs. Posts that are more senior are concerned with both policy development and its administration, and officers often work closely with both civil servants and politicians. This can be a very rewarding area of work. It can make a positive difference to the education of young people in a particular community.

I am an experienced teacher with over twenty years' teaching experience. At present I am a head of department in a secondary school and also teach in the special educational needs department. I started off my career, however, as an English teacher. I have also had experience as a further education tutor in English and local history. I am now looking for a career change and am attracted to the idea of teaching basic skills. Is there any way I could retrain for this?

Since 1 September 2002 the following requirements have applied to *new* teachers of adult literacy and numeracy:

- Teachers of adult literacy will be required to work towards both the new level 4 Certificate for Adult Literacy Subject Specialists and a full teaching qualification meeting the FENTO Teaching and Learning Standards, such as a Certificate in Education (Cert. Ed.) or a Postgraduate Certificate in Education (PGCE).
- Teachers of adult numeracy will be required to work towards both the new level 4 Certificate for Adult Numeracy Subject Specialists and a full teaching qualification meeting the FENTO Teaching and Learning Standards such as a Cert. Ed. or a PGCE.
- Teachers already qualified with a Cert. Ed. or PGCE wishing to be specialist teachers of adult literacy or numeracy will need to complete the Certificate for Adult Literacy/Numeracy Subject Specialists at level 4.
- All post-16 teachers of other subjects or vocational areas will be required to follow teacher training programmes that include coverage of the subject specifications for literacy and numeracy at level 3.

You should contact the Basic Skills Agency on 020 7405 4017 or their Helpline Number on 020 7421 2362, or your local further education college, for further information about possible courses that would suit your needs and would fit in with your current work patterns.

I am a 30-year-old unqualified English teacher currently working in a Japanese university. As well as teaching, I am also working on materials development projects; specifically, writing textbooks. I would like to transfer these skills to a career in the United Kingdom. To that end, I'm considering applying for an MA in TESOL [teaching English to speakers of other languages]. However, I am worried that all that's available after the MA is very low-paid ESL jobs, which I could get just as easily with a four-week TEFL [teaching English as a foreign language] certificate. I'd like to know about the possible career progression in TESOL and what kind of salary I could hope to earn.

Sadly, salaries in many areas of the TESOL/TEFL market tend to be very poor. There are some private-sector providers happy to pay as little as they can get away with in what has traditionally been a seller's market, with many 'teachers' opting for a short four-week training course. They then teach either part-time, or for a short while before moving on to something else. Career progression is often limited to posts such as Directors of Studies or other management positions. Some tutors set up their own businesses to work with clients they know in the commercial world. The best salaries are often in the state-regulated education sector, but such posts tend to be limited in number and hard to find. I doubt that the MA will enhance your earning power significantly, and you should work out the full costs of taking any training, and the likely benefits, both personal and financial, before embarking on the course.

I am currently in the last year of a three-year contract, teaching art in an international school. When I return to the United Kingdom I would like to work with children with emotional or behavioural difficulties or in a young offenders' institution. How might I go about this? Should I return to mainstream teaching first? And will my credibility as a classroom teacher have been affected by my time in the private sector?

You are really posing two sets of questions. First, will your time overseas have affected your credibility? The answer should be 'no', but it will partly depend upon how you sell yourself. What have you gained from the past three years teaching abroad? You may have worked with many different cultures and artistic traditions, both native to the country you are working in and contributed to by your pupils, who may have come from all over the world. In addition, have you kept up with developments in curriculum and assessment techniques in schools in the United Kingdom? Do you, for instance, teach on an International GCSE programme?

Second, you want to change direction and teach in either a special school or a young offenders' institution. You do not say why this is, or what you have done to help equip yourself for such a change. If it is just a desire to work with a different type of young person, it might be better to return to mainstream teaching and undertake some professional development. This would enhance your understanding of the needs of these groups, who can be both very demanding and very rewarding to teach. However, many special schools often have staffing vacancies and you might well be able to find a teaching job straight away. It would be up to you to decide whether you were ready for it.

I'm looking to further my career in education, but I don't want to follow the deputy/head route. Rather, I would prefer to work in supporting schools and teachers. How do I go about finding vacancies for this type of work?

Most local authority posts are advertised in the *TES,* after the teaching vacancies. Often these posts are linked to specific funding and may be time-limited in nature. There is no specific career preparation, but several years of successful teaching, some leadership experience and a record of professional development are probably prerequisites. Many of these posts are recruited from local teachers through informal networks, so knowing who are the local movers and shakers is helpful. With the role of local authorities possibly diminishing further, more of these types of posts may find their way into the private sector, just as inspections were privatised a decade ago. Do remember that once you are out of the classroom you will lose the day-to-day contact with pupils and will be working mainly with adults. Some teachers enjoy the change, others don't. So, before making the switch out of the classroom, ask yourself why you find this type of work attractive. You will also find yourself on a different set of pay and conditions, and you may no longer be eligible to remain in the Teachers' Pension Scheme.

I have been teaching for ten years and am looking to broaden my experience. Are there any risks in taking a job with a local authority?

If schools have undergone a period of rapid change, then so have local authorities and their children's services. Normally, I would say a post with a local authority was as safe as a post in a school. They are both public-sector jobs. However, you might have to change your terms and conditions of employment. You should certainly look at the implications for your pension of any change of sector. In the end, it will be the job that matters the most, but it is worth remembering that those parts of the public sector without pay review bodies have done less well in the past decade than those such as teachers whose pay is regulated by a review body.

I work part-time for personal reasons so that I can use the rest of the week to pursue my career as a writer. At present I teach adults English and some basic skills courses. I would be interested in teaching English literature in prisons. How do I go about finding out whether there is a post available in my area?

There is no central database of such jobs. Sometimes they are advertised in the *TES,* both in the main jobs section and in FE Focus. However, your first step should be to consider whether you are prepared to move to a different area if a job is available, or whether that would be too unsettling for your work as a writer. Otherwise, consider what prisons and young offenders' institutions may be within travelling distance of where you currently live, and then try to find out who is responsible for providing the education courses at each of them. However, don't forget that changing your type of teaching will be stressful, and could impact on your writing; on the other hand, it could also give you some new insights. You should weigh up the pros and cons and decide what is really motivating you at present.

I am considering taking six months out after eleven years in teaching. I am a head of year. My concern is that I will struggle to get another job as I am too expensive and that such time out will be viewed as suspicious.

An alternative would be to look for a secondment or exchange while your present school keeps your post open for a period of time. This would overcome the problem of having a post to return to, at least in theory. However, in a time of falling rolls, no post is entirely secure. Finding a new post may depend upon the added value you have generated during the time away from your present post. Basically, just taking a break may prove difficult, whereas having a definite plan of what you want to do can be positive. You can learn new skills or teach in a different location.

I would like to eventually work as an educational consultant. What training would I need?

There are no formal training programmes to become a consultant. You do need the ability to work on your own, and some experience that is marketable. Many large organisations such as the National College for School Leadership employ people in particular roles similar to consultancy. Traditionally, in education, consultancy is seen as something provided by those with expertise. The same does not apply in the industrial and commercial world, where consultants offer some of the same sort of functions that Ofsted inspections provide within the education world. Your best bet is to talk with some existing consultants about the pros and cons of their work. Any work of this nature is likely to be risky, and your income can fluctuate even in a good year. However, with many large commercial organisations moving into the education marketplace, this is an area of work that may well expand and take over some of the activities formerly provided by local authorities.

How do I find work as a researcher in education? Ever since I did my Master's degree I have wanted to stop teaching and find out more about new methods of teaching and learning.

Being a researcher is often a precarious and not very well-paid existence. However, it can be very rewarding as well. You spend time looking at areas that interest you, at least in theory. In practice, the work follows the money, and those with the purse strings may not want to research the topics that interest you. This is why so many researchers are employed on temporary contracts. Their skills may not fit the next project. You may find more reward as an amateur researcher working on topics that will pay dividends within your own school than in giving up teaching altogether. If you want to know more, the British Educational Research Association (BERA) is the main body that brings together researchers in education. It holds an annual conference each September in a different part of the country, where researchers at all levels showcase their latest projects.

5 Can I teach where I want?

Access to education is a universal human right and teachers are in demand across the world. However, there are some restrictions, and it is worth considering how any move will fit into your longer-term career plan. There is a worldwide movement of international schools, and many teachers trained in Britain are to be found working in such schools on every continent. Indeed, some teachers make a career working in such schools, as it provides an opportunity to experience different parts of the world. For some, returning home can become a problem, and if that is your eventual aim, you should have a strategy in mind to make a return possible.

I have been teaching in England for some years but my partner has been transferred to a job in Wales. Will my teaching qualification be acceptable there these days?

At present, anyone who trained in England or Wales as a teacher can move freely between teaching posts in either country. However, jobs are often more difficult to come by in Wales than in many parts of England, so you may find the competition very tough for many posts, especially in the primary sector. As the Welsh Assembly develops an education policy that is different from that in England, job swapping in either direction may become more difficult, even if there are no legal barriers in the way. Curiously, as the United Kingdom is increasingly coming to resemble a federated state, you would have more employment rights if you were going to another EU country. The Directive on the Free Movement of Labour does not apply within member states, even when they are federated states, as teachers trying to move between England and Scotland have sometimes found to their cost when trying to register their qualifications.

I've applied for a job in a secondary school, but my qualifications are related to further education teaching (I have a PGCE). I have ten years' teaching experience and teach the subject to Years 10 and 11 from local schools. If I were offered the job, would the school be obliged to appoint me on the unqualified scale, or can it decide to pay me Main Scale salary, based on merit? The job description made no mention of QTS [qualified teacher status] being a condition of employment.

Although you do not make it clear in your question, I assume you have been teaching pupils from Years 10 and 11 in the further education environment under some form of link scheme. If that is the case, then you will probably not have qualified teacher status, which would have allowed you to be paid straight away as a qualified teacher in a school setting. However, do not despair, as, if appointed, you can apply to be retrained by the school through the Graduate or Registered Teacher Programmes. The latter is for those without a degree but with the equivalent of two years' worth of higher education, such as an HND or Dip. H.E. As you have a PGCE, and have taught school-aged pupils, the programme of work should not be too onerous. Strictly speaking, if you are not being retrained, you should be employed as an instructor. Schools are only supposed to employ such staff where no qualified teacher is available, and then only until one becomes available. However, it is not clear what steps schools have to take to prove that they have tried to find a qualified teacher, or even who is responsible for checking that they have done so. Additionally, under a Statutory Instrument (SI 1663) passed by Parliament in September 2003, the definition of a 'teacher' was widened significantly so that it now probably includes people such as you.

I have been teaching in the independent sector for some years. Although I have two-thirds of an Open University degree, I have never completed it and graduated. In addition, I have done some modules on teacher training but do not have a qualification. I would now like to switch to teaching adults in the further education sector. What are my chances?

You do not say what you would like to teach, or why you want to switch sectors. Any potential employer will want to test your motivation for making such a move. Although you may not need a degree to teach in further education, you will probably find the lack of one a handicap. Also, the lack of any training qualification for working with adults probably won't help either. Perhaps your best bet would be to finish your degree while making contact with the head of the appropriate department at your local college to see whether you could discuss the possibility of a career change. Frankly, unless you have some expertise that is in demand, you may find it hard to make the switch.

I trained as a teacher in Jamaica and recently moved to England. I now want to start teaching in secondary schools here. When I was in Jamaica, I taught mathematics at all levels: from Years 6 to 13, for almost six years. So far I have sent applications to various schools without success. I have just completed a Master's degree in economics. I would appreciate your advice as to the most efficient way of getting into the classroom in Britain, and really, a paying teaching job.

I am sorry that you haven't found it easy to start teaching in England. The spring is not always a good time to be looking for a permanent post since most schools have few reasons to create new teaching jobs either at Christmas or Easter. However, despite recent worries about funding, there are still teaching posts available for September.

Two possible avenues for you to explore are, first, talking with the Recruitment Strategy Managers in the local authorities where you are looking for teaching posts. They may be able to suggest schools with potential vacancies. Alternatively, they may have schools that would be prepared to help you convert your present teaching qualification through the Overseas Trained Teacher Scheme. This scheme would give you qualified teacher status (QTS), and demonstrate that you were familiar with the National Curriculum and current teaching methods. Possession of QTS may make you more attractive to schools looking for staff.

Second, at the same time, you could contact one or more of the supply agencies that cover schools in the areas where you want to work. Supply teaching is no easy option, but it would allow you to get a foot in the door. A supply agency may also know of schools that would be willing to help you gain QTS. They might also be willing to help you make the most of your CV.

With both an economics degree and a mathematics qualification, you could also consider further education as a possible option. You don't need QTS to start work in the further education sector. There is often part-time work available, and you might find that a number of colleges would be willing to offer you a few hours' work. However, it might be in the evenings. Once again, with many courses finishing soon after Easter, this is not the best time of year to be job hunting.

I am a PE teacher and have just recently completed my training through the Graduate Training Programme, and currently I have just started my QTS year in the same school. I have always wanted to teach for a year or so in the United States (particularly in Minnesota). I was wondering what are the requirements to teach there. What processes would I have to go through, and what options are open to me?

First you might consider an exchange; look at the British Council website for details (http://www.britishcouncil.org/learning-fulbright.htm). There is also a dedicated page on the TeacherNet website (http://www.teachernet.gov.uk) that lists a variety of exchange programmes. At present, the DfES is keen to encourage internationalism. Alternatively, look out for the Visit USA adverts in the back pages of the *TES*. Visit USA is a placement agency. I am not sure whether it covers Minnesota, though. If there are any private or international schools in Minnesota (unlikely in Duluth, but possible in Minneapolis/St Paul) they might hire overseas teachers. However, you would need a visa and a green card. Each state has its own certification process, so there is no easy way to crack the United States. You could try looking at some of the job websites across the United States and see what they say about employing out-of-state teachers. Apart from exchanges, which can be with schools anywhere, you are most likely to find a teaching post in one of the big cities.

I'm a 37-year-old secondary teacher of ICT and have been teaching for three years. Now I have started to question where I am going in education, even if I were to change schools. I now believe that teaching abroad would widen both my expertise and knowledge. I also feel that with my varied background I would be able to offer more than just an ICT teacher, I have often thought that I might be suited to a teaching contract in an underprivileged school, maybe somewhere in the Third World. I would also like to rent my house out when I am away. Is there a facility where prospective teachers can post for accommodation needs?

Apart from one-year exchanges, there are broadly two types of teaching abroad experience: either working in international schools, often with privileged pupils who are part of the expat community or children of affluent locals, or working in state schools that educate children in less well-off communities. Jobs for the first group of schools are often advertised in the back pages of the *TES* and on the web. Most of those working in the second type of school do so through volunteer programmes; those often pay only the equivalent of a local wage. VSO or the British Council websites might be places to look for more information. Do remember that your pension will be affected if you teach overseas.

I don't know of any central website for teachers who want to rent out their house. You could advertise at your local university teacher training department or circulate local schools that might be employing newly qualified teachers, but it would be a bit hit and miss.

I have been a primary school teacher for seven years and I am interested in teaching abroad for a year. I have heard of an exchange scheme between schools in Scotland and Australia. Could you please provide more details and contact information.

I cannot find any specific exchange scheme between Australia and Scotland. However, you might want to look at this link from the GTC Scotland to the British Council site: http://www.cpdregister.org.uk/Links/britcounlinks.htm. Also, you might want to check out the Australian sites listed below for further information. I have no doubt that further internet searches will uncover additional links.

Information about teacher exchange can be found on EdNA Online under the category Teacher Exchange Programmes, at http://www.edna.edu.au/edna/browse/0,14774.

For information about teaching in Australia, please visit the following resource, developed by the Commonwealth Department of Education, Science and Training: http://www.dest.gov.au/noosr/leaflets/teaching_leaflet_new.htm.

Information about graduate studies in Australia, for students from overseas, can be found on EdNA Online under the category International/Students State & Territory Services at http://www.edna.edu.au/edna/browse/0,16419.

In addition, you may be interested in visiting the website of the Commonwealth Department for Education, Science and Training – International Education, at http://www.dest.gov.au/edu/internat_index.htm.

6 What are my rights?

At present, most teachers are employees. As such, they have both rights and responsibilities. This is why membership of a professional association is important, since governments often make changes to the law that will affect teachers and their careers. It is not just the current changes to the age at which a teacher can draw their full pension that you need to consider; there are frequent changes to many aspects of a teacher's pay and conditions. Some of these, such as changes in maternity or paternity leave, result from alterations in general employment legislation, whereas others, such as the determination of which posts are covered by the directed time agreement, are specific to teachers and are contained in the annual Teachers' Pay and Conditions document issued by the DfES (www.teachernet.gov.uk). This is supplemented by local agreements that cover additional matters such as time off for compassionate reasons or for graduations or moving house.

I am a qualified teacher and hold QTS [qualified teacher status], but my subject is English and at some point I would really like to get back to my first love history – but I did not do the subject at degree level and am wondering if an Open University degree would be held in the same respect as a more traditional degree. Would I need to do another PGCE [Postgraduate Certificate in Education] after doing a history degree to be able then to teach history if I already have a PGCE in English?

Although you trained in a particular subject for your PGCE, your QTS is not subject specific. You can both ask and be asked to teach other subjects. Obviously, you will be able to do this better, and to a higher level, with a degree in the subject. I don't see any problem with a degree undertaken through the route of part-time or distance learning compared with one studied over three years full-time. You won't receive any additional funding, so you will have to pay full fees for any second degree. However, there is no shortage of history teachers, so it might be worth talking to the head of history at your school about whether there is any possibility of your taking some Key Stage 3 classes; but, of course, your own department might be reluctant to let you make the switch.

Last year I was banned from driving for twelve months after being caught driving over the limit the morning after the Christmas party. Will this affect my career?

As you are aware, teachers are required to reveal any criminal convictions to their employers. Generally, these days, this means that schools have to obtain a printout from the Criminal Records Bureau when teachers change employers. However, teachers must not wait until an employer discovers any conviction; they have a duty to inform their head of any conviction. A failure to do so might in itself constitute a criminal offence. As to whether a conviction for drink driving, with its associated ban on driving for at least twelve months, would affect a teacher's career, much would depend upon the nature of the teacher's work. A classroom teacher who had never needed to learn to drive the school minibus might be inconvenienced by having to carry piles of marking on the bus, or stay later to mark them at school, but it wouldn't affect them unduly. On the other hand, a teacher who was required to drive teams to matches with other schools on a regular basis might be in a different position.

The offence will stay on a teacher's record for the rest of their career, and will need to be disclosed any time a new post is applied for. Some governing bodies might regard it as a hindrance while others would be less bothered, particularly if there were no further incidents. However, it is always better to try to be safe rather than sorry. Additionally, these days the GTC (General Teaching Council) may wish to consider whether the conviction will affect your registration and might call you to attend a hearing.

There is an in-service day that I need to attend for a new post in a different school that I will be taking up in September. My present head doesn't want to let me go, because of the supply cover costs. Can I request the day off? Alternatively, should I throw a 'sickie'?

In the days when budgets were less under pressure, a school might have been willing to fund your INSET day as a gesture of goodwill. Clearly, that doesn't seem be an option for you. Have you approached your new head to ask whether your new school will reimburse your current school for the cost of the supply cover? If it is really important that you attend, that would seem to be the best option. If there is a local agreement about 'time off' for various activities, that might also cover the situation. If not, then you will either have to miss the event, or offer to pay all the costs, including the cost of cover, yourself.

Don't take a 'sickie'. If it were proved you were attending an INSET event and not genuinely ill, you would, at the very least, lose a day's pay, and you could be considered to be acting in such a manner as to have broken your contract. It just isn't worth the risk.

I am applying for a job. At present I have had several interviews, but have always come second. Is there any restriction on the number of interviews that I can attend?

You will need to check whether there are any locally agreed terms and conditions about days off that have been negotiated between the professional associations and your employers. Generally, one would expect the term 'reasonable' to be used if there is such an agreement. However, that is always difficult to define. Normally, if there is no agreement, it would be down to common sense. If you are always coming second, then you are clearly not being frivolous and just wasting time. On the other hand, it will become frustrating to you if you are always the runner-up and never the winner. You might want to see whether there is any thread running through debriefs you may have had. Are you perhaps aiming a bit too high for your experience, or have you just been unlucky? If you can, talk it through with your head. They will clearly know by now that you are aiming to leave and may be able to offer some insight into why you are being unsuccessful.

I am thinking of going to work overseas for a couple of years; how will this affect my pension?

The Teachers' Pension Scheme is intended for those who work in maintained schools and colleges in England and Wales. However, some non-maintained schools are also members. I don't believe that any of them are overseas schools. The only exception might be the small number of EU schools run by national governments primarily for those who work in the various organisations, paid for by the European Commission. The school in England is located in Culham, near Oxford, close to a number of scientific projects.

If you go to work for any other school overseas you should certainly ask whether it has a pension plan; if so, you should take advice about making contributions. If there is no scheme, you should seek professional advice about the options open to you. Much will depend upon how you are paid. One option to ask about is the feasibility of putting money aside into a savings account and then buying-in extra years when you resume teaching in Britain. However, pension regulations are a very complicated area and you do need to consider taking expert advice. In the first instance you should contact your own professional association for help.

I keep seeing pay scales labelled 'Inner London'. However, nobody I talk to seems to know where Inner London starts and ends. I am training in south London and wonder how this will affect where I look for a teaching post.

Nearly thirty years ago, during a teacher supply crisis, the boundaries that decide which teachers should receive the Inner London Allowance were set. All schools in nineteen of the London boroughs qualify for what is now known as the 'Inner London Pay Scale'. Apart from the obvious places such as Westminster and Islington, schools in areas like Barking and Dagenham and Brent qualify, but those in boroughs such as Waltham Forest or Kingston do not. However, they would still qualify for additional salary on the Outer London Scale. There is also the London Fringe area, which is slightly further out, where teachers are also paid on a higher salary than in the rest of the country. Some schools near the boundaries of the different salary areas may use Recruitment and Retention Allowances to offset the difference between their basic salary levels and those in neighbouring schools within the higher pay areas. A full list of local areas where schools are within the different pay areas is given in the Teachers' Pay and Conditions document. In April 2005 the Outer London and London Fringe Allowances were replaced by separate pay scales. From that date, there have effectively been four pay scales for teachers in England and Wales: Inner London, Outer London, the London Fringe Area and the remainder of England and Wales. This change, by replacing allowances with pay scales, opens the door to the introduction of a wider system of regional pay, if the government is so minded, at some point in the future.

My head has told me that, owing to a cash shortage, the school cannot afford to employ anyone to do our photocopying. I thought this was one of the tasks mentioned in the Workload Agreement. Can I force my head to find someone to do my photocopying?

Bulk photocopying of work, such as class sets, is one of the tasks covered by the Workload Agreement. This means that teachers are not required to do this task, and the school should have put a structure in place that allows it to be carried out for you. This is a statutory requirement and cannot be avoided because the school has a budget crisis.

Do note that the agreement covers only 'bulk' copying, so you will still be expected to do the odd bit of photocopying that might arise when you are researching for lessons. There is also the question of what happens if the person responsible for photocopying is absent. Normally, the school will make alternative arrangements, but in the short term you might be expected to do your own copying. Don't expect to rush in at lunch time and demand several sets of photocopying for that afternoon's lessons. Most schools will have a system in place that requires some notice. If you leave your lesson planning to the last minute you might still find yourself chained to the photocopier.

Could you please give me a quick rundown of the grievance and complaints procedures for staff in schools? Or a website that will give me this information. My school does not have such a procedure and apparently follows the national one.

Your local trade unions will no doubt have agreed a procedure with the local authority. I am sure it will have been referred to in the employee's contract of employment that was given to you when you started work at the school.

However, a new procedure came into force from October 2004. Employers and employees will be required to follow, as a minimum, a three-stage process to ensure that disputes are first discussed at work. The process requires the problem to be set out in writing, with full details provided to the other party; both parties meet to discuss the problem; and an appeal is arranged if requested.

Use of these procedures is set out in regulations flowing from the Employment Act 2002. The regulations require all employers to have procedures in place to deal with disputes, so in most circumstances, employees will not be able to make claims to employment tribunals about grievances unless they have formally raised a grievance at work first; but employers who dismiss staff without using the statutory procedure will normally be guilty of unfair dismissal. As this is an area where there are frequent changes to the law, do check for the current position on the DTI website at www.dti.gov.uk.

I am an NQT. I have obtained a PGCE to teach at primary level but I am also applying to high schools to teach religious education and the humanities. Unfortunately, I have not managed to obtain a permanent position and am currently doing supply teaching. Whenever I approach a school regarding long-term supply I run into a problem. As the evenings are drawing in, I need to go home early on Friday afternoon, as Shabbat comes in at 3.30p.m. for a number of weeks. I have tried all the local Jewish schools and am now trying to find work in a non-Jewish school.

I am sorry that your faith is proving a barrier to your employment as a teacher. As Britain becomes a multi-faith community, issues such as yours are becoming more likely to arise. Historically, Jewish teachers and those of other faiths were normally allowed time off for major religious festivals that fell during the school terms. You could try to negotiate a part-time contract for nine-tenths of the week, finishing at lunchtime on Fridays. This might be more acceptable to a school than trying to timetable your non-contact time for Friday afternoons, even if you were to disappear early only for about a quarter of the school year.

However, EU member states have signed up to the Directive on Equal Treatment in Employment. Under this directive, unjustifiable discrimination in the employment of individuals on the grounds of their religious beliefs is an infringement of human rights and, at the same time, an infringement of individual religious liberty. New regulations came into force in December 2003 in Britain, entitled the Employment Equality (Religion or Belief) Regulations 2003. More details can be found on the website http://www.dti.gov.uk/employment/discrimination/religion-belief/index.html. It may well be that a school cannot ask about your religious beliefs before appointing you, unless it is a faith school, and employers may also have to meet your need to be at home by the time darkness falls on a Friday. You should consult your professional association for more details.

Is it possible to get out of parents' evenings and the twelve-hour day they involve whilst I am pregnant? We have a parents' evening and two open evenings coming up before the end of term. My head says that I can only miss the parents' evenings if I manage to ring all the parents personally to discuss student's progress. That seems unreasonable, as it will take me months to get to speak to sixty parents during the day.

This is a tricky issue. Reporting to parents is a central part of a teacher's role, and that generally includes the possibility of face-to-face meetings. With so many parents working these days, they often need to be held in the evenings. However, you have your own welfare to consider. Arranging to contact parents by phone and booking telephone appointments might be regarded as an administrative task, although it is not specifically mentioned in the list produced by the DfES. Under the Workload Agreement, schools are required to consider the work–life balance of a teacher's job. It would be best to see whether you can find a compromise. Written feedback with the possibility of a telephone conversation for those who want it is one possibility. It should be booked on the night of the parents' evening. Then you would only need to speak to those parents who really wanted a conversation about their offspring's progress.

I am in my late thirties and completed my NQT [newly qualified teacher] year on a temporary contract that was not renewed because of falling rolls at the school. There are no jobs in my area, so I went into supply teaching until something turns up. I want to know what pension rights I have, if any, and what I have to do about it.

I am sorry that you have not found a teaching post after completing your period as an NQT. Your query is about pension rights. Your first port of call is to the supply agency that employs you, to ask what arrangements it makes. Second, you should investigate the government's stakeholder pension scheme. It may be that if you are placed in a school for one term, and the school pays your salary, you will be eligible to join the Teachers' Pension Scheme. When you finally find a teaching post you should certainly consider joining that scheme and take advice on whether you are able to import any existing pension provision you have made during your earlier working career, and the relative merits of so doing. Finally, avoid the temptation to do nothing. If all else fails, ask yourself, can I put some of my income aside each week? The longer you can save for retirement, the better off you will be in the end.

Does the sick pay year still run from April to April? If so, does that mean that someone in their third year of teaching could be on full pay all autumn term, half pay all spring term and back on full pay for summer term? I am off ill and do not know when I will be better. I need to plan for next year. In addition, can I apply for statutory sick pay once I am on half pay?

The so-called sick leave year does run from 1 April to 31 March the following year, thus following the financial year fairly closely. However, your length of service as a teacher normally determines your entitlement to sick pay. There are nationally agreed minimum entitlements, but some authorities may be more generous. If you are absent owing to illness on 31 March, you will not be entitled to the subsequent year's allowance until you have recovered and are back at work. Instead, sick leave will continue to count against the previous year's entitlement.

To take your example, a teacher in their third year of service will normally be entitled to full pay for seventy-five working days and half pay for a further seventy-five days. Thus, if they went sick at the start of term in September, they would exhaust their full pay after fifteen weeks and their half pay after a further fifteen weeks, excluding holiday periods. However, they would not be able to return to full pay until after they had returned to work and started the 'clock' running again. They would probably be required to attend a medical examination in these circumstances.

As statutory sick pay (SSP) is payable only for a maximum of twenty-eight weeks, a teacher in their third year of service could receive SSP for thirteen weeks while on half pay. When sick pay runs out after twenty-eight weeks, and there is no agreement about an infirmity or a breakdown pension, then a teacher should be eligible to claim state incapacity benefit. As this is a complicated issue, you should contact your professional association about the details.

I teach at an international school. We have real problems with the head, who appointed his wife to the staff. His wife has been verbally, racially and physically abusing children and has been protected by him. The parents now know and she may be dismissed, but the governors are still supporting the head. Crucially, we know, and have evidence, that similar events took place in two previous schools, one in Somerset and one in Paris, with the two of them eventually being dismissed. Our governors are ignoring this evidence. My school is the latest victim. Is there any agency we can appeal to? What can we do to stop this happening at the next school they go to?

Much will depend upon what type of school you are working in. The country where it is located will also make a difference. Some schools are businesses run for profit by their owners, who may also be the head teacher. Others are charitable foundations where all staff including the head as well as other teachers, are appointed by a board of governors. Yet others have some variation of one of these two main types.

The answer to your question is, therefore, more complicated than it might be. First, if no legal charges of abuse have been proved, you should be very careful about what you say or write, unless you can support it with clear evidence. In an owner-controlled school that is operated as a profit-making business, there is probably nothing to stop the owner appointing their partner to the staff. In other schools the governing body has a duty to ensure that normal recruitment practices have been followed. However, in many countries employment law may be less well developed than in Europe or North America. This might be something for the international bodies that accredit these schools to consider. A 'whistle-blowing' agreement that schools signed up to might be a first step, but it would be very difficult to enforce. In the end, the criminal law must be invoked where there is any abuse that breaks the law of whatever country the school is located in.

I have just accepted a two-year secondment from my school to work with a local authority project. The salary is slightly lower than my present teaching salary, but the experience will be worth it, and the school is willing to keep my teaching post open for the two years. However, I have been told that my pension is to be transferred to the local government scheme. Do I have to agree to this?

Without knowing the whole terms of your contract and the arrangement between the school and the local authority, it is difficult to comment in any detail on your query. However, there are some questions that you might want to ask. If it is a genuine secondment, and the school is receiving the full cost of your employment, why does your position need to change? However, it might be that the school is not charging for your services, but in effect lending you for two years to the authority. In that case the authority may see this as a post falling within its pension scheme. However, you should ask whether the post could also qualify for inclusion within the Teacher's Pension Scheme. The decision may be affected by whether you are required to have a different holiday and work pattern as compared with teachers. Although you could almost certainly return to the teacher's scheme when you come back to teaching in two years' time, you do need to clear up issues about who is actually your employer for the next two years and whether your period of 'continuous service' is affected. It might never matter, but it is always better to be safe than sorry. Your union should be able to give you more detailed advice.

I teach in a small primary school for half the week on a temporary contract. There is a gap between lessons that I am not paid for. If I am asked to work this period, say to cover for an absent colleague, then I am offered time off in lieu. However, I would rather be paid. Is there anything that I can do about the situation?

This is a matter for negotiation between you and the school. Convoluted contracts of this type have become more common as schools have tried to save money by paying part-time teachers only for the work they are doing. In the end, the relationship between teachers and schools is much like a marketplace. If you can find a better deal somewhere else, you are free to take it. If you cannot, you have to make the best of what is on offer. However, in 2006 the School Teachers' Pay Review Body will consider the whole issue of part-time teachers and their pay and conditions of service. What once looked a generous package has been eroded by both the parsimony of some schools and changes in employment law following the outcome of a series of legal cases in Europe.

When I was a young teenager I was cautioned for shoplifting with a friend (even though I never actually stole anything). I am now 22 and through teacher training have had clearance from the Criminal Records Bureau [CRB]. Does this mean that the caution has gone from my record? I am really worried, as I am starting to look for teaching posts and don't want to put it on my form. I have not mentioned it in the past in connection with other jobs and nothing has ever come back to me. Does this mean I can finally forget about the whole incident?

Failure to disclose a conviction, including a caution, could be a criminal offence in certain circumstances. However, now that the CRB has been established, your employer will be required to check with it when you apply for a teaching post. If anything is known, it will be divulged and should be shown to you. The CRB website contains a page dealing with your rights to information: http://www.disclosure.gov.uk/Default. aspx?page=291. It may be that the caution was never recorded officially. Personally, I believe that these types of cautions, reprimands and final warnings issued to young people under 16 should normally be regarded as a spent conviction in most cases where there has been no further offending after the age of 16. But until you can clear up whether the caution was ever officially recorded against your name, you will need to declare it. I would be surprised if, by itself, it would hamper your search for a teaching post.

I accepted a new job at the start of May and have resigned from my current job. When I applied for my new post I stated that I had no convictions and sent a check done in March with my acceptance letter and ID. I have subsequently found that I was convicted in April (in another county) of driving with no tax and insurance. I have not intentionally deceived my new employer in any way and this is really due to a chapter of (admittedly negligent) accidents. What shall I do? I am really concerned that my employer will not want to employ me any more.

You should be honest with the new school and explain all the facts. At the same time, write to the court that imposed the fine and points in your absence, saying you had documentation and asking whether the case can be reopened now you are aware of the summons, because you were not guilty of the offences. (This assumes that you just forgot to comply with the seven-day notice to produce the documents that the police officer gave you. As you did not receive the summons, the court may be willing to reconsider the case for you.) If your documents were all in order, you might not end up with a criminal record after all.

I am looking at applying for a new post at another school to start in September. When is the last date that I can resign from my present post?

Normally, it is three months or the end of May for jobs starting in September, and two months at other times. However, these dates can be flexible if both schools agree. This is sometimes, but not always, more likely if they are in the same authority.

Some teachers walk out giving little or no notice. Although it may seem a good thing to do at the time, it will almost certainly prejudice what the school might write in any future reference that you ask it to provide.

I am currently employed on a full-time permanent contract as an ICT teacher at a secondary comprehensive school. I am leaving my current post at the end of the autumn term, and wonder what holiday pay I am entitled to. I was under the impression it would be for the full two-week holiday, but the headmaster seems to think that we are paid in 'segments' and that I am therefore entitled to pay only until 31 December.

If you are on permanent contract, you can expect to be paid up until 31 December. This is assuming that you gave the required period of at least two months' notice. There is sometimes confusion because of the use of the word 'term' in respect of the notice period, and your pay. For pay purposes, the year is divided into three terms. If you were starting a new teaching job in a maintained school, you would expect to be paid from 1 January. However, if you are leaving teaching, it will be up to your new employer when your new job will start. There is sometimes greater confusion about what happens at Easter. The spring term runs from 1 January to 30 April. If you are leaving teaching, it is possible for you to be required to return until 30 April. For teachers moving schools, this would not normally happen.

As the union rep I have been asked by my colleagues to find out if PPA [planning, preparation and assessment] time has to be used to attend courses. For instance, in our school we all receive the same afternoon each week. If a course falls on the same day as our PPA time, can PPA time be rearranged so that we still receive our 10 per cent release time? We currently have to miss our weekly PPA time if a course has been booked.

This is something of an uncertain area that needs to be fully tested. According to the Pay and Conditions Document, PPA time should be used for just that purpose. Staff development is a professional duty, along with teaching and attending staff meetings. On this basis, if you cannot be required either to teach or to attend staff meetings in your PPA times, you should not be required to attend staff development activities. That said, in schools that are functioning effectively as a team, staff might be prepared to forgo their PPA time if there were a cogent reason for the activity to take place at that time – perhaps the availability of a speaker. I don't think management can assume that they can regularly encroach on PPA time for other sorts of activities, however worthy or important they are.

I have been signed off work with glandular fever since about six weeks ago – I am off till January but was asked to see my doctor again before I went back. I started teaching in September 2003 at an independent school. This year in September I moved to a state school and am doing my training as well. I am not sure how many days of full pay I am entitled to; does it start from September 2003 or this September? I would appreciate it if you could enlighten me.

I am sorry to hear you are off work with glandular fever. Assuming you started teaching at the beginning of September, you will still not have completed one term's service. Although there are generous national terms for teachers' sick pay, that most local authorities adhere to, they are graduated on your length of service. Thus teachers with less than four months' service will receive twenty-five working days on full pay. After four months' service you would also have been entitled to an additional seventy-five days on half-pay. However, do not despair, as you are also entitled to statutory sick pay (SSP). This is paid to any employee for a maximum period of twenty-eight weeks in any spell of sickness absence. It is paid after taking into account any other pay received: it is not paid for the twenty-five days for which you receive full pay. If you are still unable to work after the twenty-eight weeks are up, you may be entitled to state incapacity benefit. Your employer may have discretion to extend the length of time you receive sick pay, but unless you can make out a good case, it probably won't do so. However, if your employment ends when you are on sick pay, your benefits may also change, depending upon why you left your employment. You should seek advice on this point.

All this is based upon your being an employee with a proper contract of employment. I have assumed from your question that you are not on the Graduate Teacher Programme and that, therefore, you do have such a contract. If you are not, perhaps because you are on a different programme, or are actually a student, then different rules may apply. I think it unlikely that your previous service will count, but you should ask your employer. You should consult your professional association for more information.

I was in the Teachers' Pension Scheme from 1998 to the end of 2002. For three of these years I paid 5 per cent additional voluntary contributions (AVCs) to the Prudential. In 2003 I started work for the LEA and was automatically moved over to Solbury Pay Scale and into the Local Government Pension Scheme (LGPS). I haven't paid any AVCs into the LGPS scheme (yet).

I recently received information which stated that I can ask that my contributions in the Teachers' Pension Scheme be 'added into' my current LGPS. But if I want to do this, I must do it by 1 November this year.

Please can you advise me if I have interpreted this correctly and, indeed, I can amalgamate the two pensions? Also, can you advise me as to whether this is a prudent thing to do – that is, what are the advantages and disadvantages? Also, would you advise paying the maximum (AVCs) into the Local Government Pension Scheme?

Advising on pensions is a difficult and complex issue, since all circumstances are slightly different. For that reason, you will need to seek expert advice: start with your professional association, who should have a pensions expert available to answer your question. When you change jobs, it is normally possible to transfer your existing contributions into the new employer's scheme, if there is one. Generally, it is only worth transferring benefits from one scheme to another if there is no diminution in their value – that is, if the new scheme has benefits either equal to or better than those of the one you are transferring from. As we have seen, in recent years there has been much upheaval in the pension sphere. We need to save for our old age, and the earlier we start the easier it is, but savings need to be secure. The Teachers' Pension Scheme is backed by the government, whereas local authorities operate funded schemes in a similar fashion to the private sector, placing the contributions into an investment portfolio and paying pensioners out of the fund. AVCs are useful if you think you will have a break in your career at any point, as they can help make up for missing years. However, in the early stages of their careers most people cannot afford to make such additional payments into their pension scheme; it is hard enough to pay the mortgage and other bills without such an extra burden.

My head refuses to promote me because I am part-time. Is this legal?

Of course not. Have you actually applied for a post and been told you weren't offered the job because you can't work full-time? If so, talk with your professional association. However, if you haven't applied and only sounded out your head, who then expressed a preference for full-time staff, apply and see what happens. However, there are some posts where even job sharing can be challenging, such as at head of department level, where a lack of overlap between staff can make it more difficult for others. Even so, some schools still manage.

I am a deputy head and I am having problems with being on a lower wage than some of the other teachers in the school now they have moved to UPS [Upper Pay Scale] 3 (and have TLR [Teaching and Learning Responsibility] points).

The governors should review your salary each year. You should be on a five-point range taken from the Leadership Scale. The minimum point should ensure your salary is at least the next Leadership Scale pay point above the lowest-paid classroom teacher and above the minimum of any assistant head teacher employed by the school. The governing body pay staffing committee should be familiar with the rules. If they don't seem to be, try telling them to look at the Teachers' Pay and Conditions Document. You should ask whether you are entitled to back pay if you have been underpaid since last September.

My son, who is disabled, is having an operation in the near future and I need time off for this. My head is being uncooperative about it. How can I get the time off with pay? I'll either be with my son in hospital, or looking after his younger brother while my wife is at the hospital. Is there an entitlement in either of these cases? From talking with teachers at my school it appears that women staff have been granted medical time off with pay but, as the only man, I feel that I'm not receiving the same deal.

This is a complicated area of the law. Basically, you may be covered under the provisions relating to parental leave that were introduced a couple of years ago. You can find out more at http://www.dti.gov.uk/er/intguid1.htm. Curiously, I can find nothing on the DfES TeacherNet (http://dti.gov.uk/employment/workand_families/parental-leave/index.htm) about the subject, so that may be why your head is confused. Certainly, this is an area where both parents should have equal rights. If you don't feel you are being properly treated, this is an issue to take up with your professional association.

Do you know the rules on time off for a family wedding during term time? Am I entitled to paid time off or must I take leave unpaid?

The terms and conditions of your appointment will have told you in the small print where to find this information. Most local authorities have worked out long ago what they would accept as reasonable. It does vary around the country. For instance, many authorities accept that for new graduates, attending their graduation ceremony is an important day and therefore allow one day off with pay. There are similar concessions for the death of a close family member. Weddings are more difficult. Even for a close relative, such as a sibling, you might find you have to take unpaid leave, and for more remote family members even a request for unpaid leave might be regarded with some scepticism. This is one of the penalties of working in an occupation that operates a controlled form of flexitime. In the end, much will depend upon how your head feels about your request, and probably upon how you are viewed in the school. If you rarely have time off sick, and are regarded as an asset to the school, you may find such a request treated more favourably than one from a teacher who is viewed differently. But that's life, even in these days of rules and regulations.

I have two job interviews in the next few weeks. If the first school were to offer me the job and I agreed to it, but then I go to the second interview (the school I actually might prefer to work at) and they also offer me the job, can I back out of the first? There is approximately one week between the two interviews and it is the second one that I would prefer to get, but I feel grateful even to have got to interview stage, considering the lack of jobs. If I verbally agree to the first, but back out later, is this legal?

The problem is neatly summed up by the proverb 'a bird in the hand is worth two in the bush'. If you are offered the first job but not the second, there is no problem. But if you are offered the second as well as the first, can you legally pull out after being offered the first job? It certainly happens, but you might gain a reputation for unreliability. If the two schools are at opposite ends of the country, this probably won't matter much. But even above the legal issue is the moral one of being in possession of 'insider' knowledge that is unknown to one side of the transaction. You know you have another interview, but the school doesn't. Provided you can live with your conscience, this doesn't matter. But really you should either tell the school that you have another interview, or at least indicate that you want time to think about the offer. The school may not give you that luxury, and would be right to ask, why did you apply for a job at our school if you didn't really want it?

I am looking for a headship in a small primary school but am alarmed about the amount of teaching that I see is required from the adverts. Is there any maximum?

Heads of small schools have always had to juggle with paperwork, parents and class teaching. Over the years, as the job has become more complicated, and the services of local authorities more distant, heads have acquired some clerical help. However, the 10,000 or so heads in schools with fewer than 100 pupils probably all have to teach for a part of the week. Generally, the maximum is no more than three days, but do ask your professional association for the latest position.

7 Leaving your job

Despite the loss of a proportion of teachers early in their careers, the majority of those who enter the profession have traditionally remained in it for most, if not all, of their working lives. Whether this will change is open to debate. There are those who believe that career paths will become more flexible, that teachers will quit for other careers, and new entrants will join the profession in mid-career. With the wide range of options open to teachers there has been the possibility of a new direction away from the classroom. However, some teachers find a new interest that will take them away from the classroom. Others will leave for family reasons either to act as carers or to work in a family business. But, for most teachers, leaving will be when retirement comes along.

After twenty years in teaching I feel like a change. Should I take the risk and quit my job? I am currently a deputy head in a small school.

To answer this question you need to know what, if any, are your remaining career goals, and why you feel you want a change. Leaving without another job to go to is always a high-risk strategy. How have you got yourself into this situation? Do you know what you want to do next? If there is something you have wanted to do for some time, and it has been nagging away at you, then your restlessness is understandable. However, ask yourself what you have to lose by making an unplanned move at this point in your career. Obviously, you will have talked the problem over with any family you have, and taken their views into account.

You can draw up a balance sheet of what you stand to gain and what you will lose by making the move you are contemplating. Only you can know what will go on either side of the ledger, but as you have already identified, there is the risk of an uncertain future to be balanced against continuing to do a job that no longer satisfies you.

Try to test the water before taking any decisive action. If you are aiming to start out on your own, using some skill or talent you have, can you do it part-time or during the holidays to see whether what is enjoyable as a sideline will be both fulfilling and financially viable as a full-time activity? Maybe a change of scene is all you need. If you have been in your school for a long time, can your head arrange a secondment to work on something like a special project?

I am thinking of applying for a new job (not teaching in a classroom, but as an education expert for a voluntary body). The post carries the same salary as teaching. It is a job I would love to do. The only problem is that the job starts in January, but the interviews are not until November this year, which means that if I got the job I wouldn't be able to accept it, as I haven't handed in my notice at school.

I never cease to be amazed by the lack of understanding about the education job market by some organisations that ought to know better. In this case, apply, and if you are awarded the post on merit as the best candidate, then negotiate about your starting date. Your school may be willing to let you go early, or the organisation may see sense once it realises it has artificially restricted the field by specifying a January start date, but not interviewing until November. There is a risk that having realised it has restricted the potential size of the field, that it could scrap the whole process and start again.

Can you give resignation in, have it accepted and the school advertise for a teacher, then change your mind?

Normally, the answer must be no; otherwise schools wouldn't know where they were. However, if you have a good reason, such as no longer having to relocate because of your partner's employment falling through, it is worth asking the head where the process of seeking your replacement has reached. If applications haven't closed, then the school might consider aborting the process. However, if your replacement has been offered and accepted a contract, you will almost certainly be out of luck. These days it is better not to resign until you are absolutely sure about your future employment.

I have been teaching for four years, and this year seems much worse than before. I no longer enjoy the job and am constantly depressed. This is not healthy for me or my family.

I am worried about leaving the security of my job, knowing that I have nothing set up for September. I expect that I could always do supply and I have until the autumn to find something new, but I know if I don't resign now I never will. I will just carry on making do, and I feel if I carry on like this I will end up making myself seriously ill.

I have decided to hand in my resignation now. I am going to see the school year out as I have exam classes, and also I am not in a financial position where I can just up and leave sooner, although I wish I were. Also it will mean I will get paid during the summer.

I wanted to ask, how do I write my letter of resignation?

I am sorry that you are no longer enjoying teaching. Work–life balance may have been the mantra of the past few years, but it still isn't easy to juggle the two. First, to the practical advice: all you need do is write your head a simple letter stating that you are resigning with effect from the 31 August. Keep any discontent or recriminations for an oral discussion, then it won't be on file. You have until the last day of May to resign, so why resign before then when you don't have another post to go on to?

By all means start looking, and even applying, for another post. You can then either resign when you have found one or reconsider if you don't find anything suitable. You are not in a position to be without a job, so don't put yourself at a disadvantage before you start looking. Consider the reaction of anyone reading a reference from your current head that started ...'X has resigned without a teaching post to move to'. Then there is your assumption that you can always do supply. Unless you are a talented teacher in a shortage subject, this may not be as easy as you think. Check out the supply teaching threads on the *TES* staffroom website. Finally, is there anyone within the school you can talk to about improving your lot in case you cannot find another job?

I completed my GTP [Graduate Teacher Programme] year in 2004, have done my NQT [newly qualified teacher] year and in July 2006 will have completed my first full year as a 'proper' teacher.

I am not currently enjoying teaching very much because I am feeling very stressed, and I am considering taking a year out of the profession to assess my feelings and maybe explore some other things.

My current thoughts are a Master's degree in a subject related to my field (design and technology) or to do something completely different such as volunteering in Africa for a few months and doing something for someone else in more need than the children I currently teach!

My concern is that if I am seen to have left teaching to pursue something unrelated and then come back to the profession, will this put me in an inferior position to other teachers who have been solidly working for several years?

I have been looking to change schools for a while and I have found it much more difficult than I imagined because I teach the niche of textiles only within the design and technology umbrella.

I am worried that I might not be seen as having enough commitment if I were to take a year away and then decide to come back.

Although you see yourself as a 'niche' teacher of textiles, you can teach across the D&T curriculum. There are more jobs for textiles/home economics than just for textiles. However, any extra advantage you can add to your CV will help. You seem undecided between some extreme choices, so it may be that you are more interested in moving away from your present choice than to anything in particular. I suggest you narrow down your choice to what you really want to do, and then take the risk, since you are clearly unhappy where you are at present.

When it comes to finding a new job, it will be the same kind of selling job you did when you found your present post, but with the added advantages of more teaching experience and whatever you have chosen to do next year. If you are going abroad, then applying for a new job will be difficult until you return home, so that may be something to take into account.

As to your being seen as having a lack of commitment, I think it depends on how you sell the experience. Schools want teachers who are positive and can explain why they did something, not just drifters.

I qualified as a teacher in 1998. I then spent two and a half years working in a school before leaving to do supply work. Over the past three years I have worked in numerous schools. The education authority that has now offered me a full-time post has decided that because of the time that I left teaching, in August 2000, it cannot put me on M3, and instead it has put me on M1 (the same as a newly qualified teacher). Surely this cannot be right?

The problem may have arisen because when you last worked for a local authority the main pay spine had nine points. During the intervening period this was reduced to six points. If you left with two years of service this would translate from the old M2 to M1 on the current pay spine. The local authority has discretion to award extra points for work 'other than as a classroom teacher', but not apparently for such work as a classroom teacher. It seems that you might indeed be better off going back to supply work unless you can find a way for the exercise of some discretion about your work over the past three years.

8 Can I come back, please?

For those who do quit the classroom, coming back still remains a problem. Too many schools do not reward experience gained outside the school gate, and some heads allegedly even feel threatened by those who have a wide range of experience. The Training and Development Agency (the former Teacher Training Agency) has been running courses for would-be 'returners' to teaching for some years, and these can provide a valuable form of re-entry. With the demand for some teachers likely to fall over the coming decade, not all who want to return will find it easy to do so. There will always be popular parts of the country where teaching posts are more in demand than in some other areas. However, all areas will still have some posts on offer. For instance, between September 2005 and the end of July 2006, just over 30,000 jobs were advertised nationally for secondary teachers. These included more than a thousand for English teachers and over 1,200 for science teachers. The full list is contained in Appendix A.

I left my position as a deputy head just under two years ago and have been working as a supply teacher ever since. At present I am looking for a full-time permanent position.

However, I am concerned that I left my last full-time post after only a term, and my former head won't speak to me. Until my last job I had an unblemished career. I was forced to leave my last post for the sake of my health, as I was diagnosed with depression. I am now fully recovered. I have good references but, in a small authority, I wonder whether heads talk unofficially to each other and whether my last head teacher may be unfairly representing me. How do I explain this episode in my career to future employers?

Despite all employment laws about how to treat people, you can never stop heads and other managers talking, especially in a small authority. You don't say whether you had worked for the same authority before your unfortunate experience, or whether you have also been a supply teacher in that authority. Either of those good experiences may help to bolster your profile with potential employers.

However, first you may wish to reflect upon what type of post you are looking for. Are you trying to return to a deputy headship or just a classroom teacher post? If the latter, then you may want to consider being candid on your application form, and say that you tried a deputy headship but found it wasn't for you, at least in that school. If your health record has always been good, and you have worked consistently as a supply teacher for the past year, say so. Also, ask whoever finds you the supply work either to act as a referee or to provide a transcript of your work record over the past year. It may be that taking a step back will allow you to move forward in the future.

It is worth talking with an adviser, or someone else from the authority, who may either know of you or be able to access accurate information on your career. You should be candid with them in asking for career advice. Also, have you undertaken any professional development in the past year? Improving your employability may make you more attractive to schools in what in some parts of the country is becoming an increasingly competitive job market.

I have an overseas QTS [qualified teacher status] in English and taught in a secondary school in London for seven years. I left teaching in 1997, when I got a doctorate in linguistics and lectured for some time abroad. I am now trying to get back into secondary teaching. I have not been able to secure a place on a refresher course. Is it worth applying for jobs straight away or should I do some supply work first, as is sometimes suggested? And how do I deal with the fact that I am overqualified? On the whole, what do you think is the best way for me to get back into teaching?

First, I should explain for those who haven't come across the term that 'overseas QTS' is granted to teachers who trained elsewhere in the European Union and have the right to work in England and Wales under the directives that relate to the 'free movement of labour'. I don't see why you feel you are overqualified. It may be that you are more qualified than before for the teaching posts you used to have, but that is not the same thing. A school ought to welcome your willingness to teach and regard you as an asset, not a nuisance. However, the additional experience and qualifications you have gained since 1997 might mean that you could now apply for posts with more responsibility, should you want to.

As to what you should do now, I would certainly apply to the local supply agencies. They know the market and can advise you. But I would also be looking at the various advertisements for teaching posts and applying for any posts that meet your criteria. You might also check that you are selling yourself in the best way on your CV. After all, many heads may not know what a teacher with overseas QTS is, and won't bother to find out.

Although I did a PGCE [Postgraduate Certificate in Education] in languages some years ago, I have never taught in Britain. Instead, I went overseas straight afterwards and taught in an EFL school, becoming a Director of Studies. I now want to work in London and wonder what my options are.

If you want to teach in the secondary sector, you may be hampered by the fact that you have never used the skills acquired during your training. However, some schools, particularly those with large numbers of non-native speakers of English, may welcome your additional expertise gained from working with those learning English. As an alternative, you could consider the further education sector, where you might be able to combine both EFL work and foreign language teaching. With a background such as yours it is worth making the first move and contacting recruitment managers in the areas where you would like to work to see whether they know of schools that would welcome your special talents.

I gained a primary PGCE in the early 1990s, but owing to personal circumstances at that time embarked upon a career away from teaching. I always regretted this, and in January this year, having updated myself with developments in the profession and undertaken classroom observations, I enrolled as a supply teacher and have worked regularly, mostly with KS2 classes since then. I now want to work full-time with a class of my own. How will an application from someone with my track record be viewed? Would I be best to continue with supply work and enrol on the next available returners' course?

Surely it doesn't have to be an 'either – or' decision at this point in time. As you have decided you want to work in one school, and have prepared yourself by doing your homework about the changes in schools since you qualified, and have undertaken some regular supply work, why not reply to any adverts you see for appropriate teaching posts? Meanwhile, you can continue with the supply work and look for the next returners' course. At this time of year you have a head start; by next summer there may be a new cohort of primary teachers leaving training and looking for teaching jobs. You can ask the heads of schools where you are working on supply if they know of any possible opening and whether they would be prepared to give you a reference.

I am currently teaching in an international school in Africa. Because my partner's job has taken him around the world, most of my teaching career has been spent in such schools, although I qualified in the United Kingdom and passed my probation in a state school about fifteen years ago. We are now set to return to London, and I wonder how hard it will be to find a teaching post, particularly as my main subject is history.

Much will depend upon when you return to England and want to start teaching, since most teaching posts are geared to a September starting date. However, applying for posts while still overseas is often problematic, and you may find little interest in any applications you make from overseas. Clearly, your experience of teaching abroad will be useful to many schools in London that, like many of the schools you will have taught in, take pupils from a wide range of different nationalities. If you have experience of teaching the National Curriculum while overseas, that is clearly a plus point, but you may not find it easy to obtain a post of responsibility straight away. The Training and Development Agency for Schools (TDA) has sponsored courses for those 'returning' to teaching and you may like to contact it to see whether you are eligible to attend such a course.

I left teaching to start a family some years ago, and have been reading recently about how this year there are more teachers than ever before in training. I am not yet ready to return to teaching, but will want to re-enter the profession in a couple of years' time. What are my chances of a job likely to be?

There are record numbers of trainee teachers this year, although still not enough in certain secondary subject areas. Primary trainees may struggle to find jobs in some parts of the United Kingdom for the next couple of years, as school rolls are falling by around 50,000 pupils a year. However, retirements on age grounds have started to rise significantly from their present levels in both primary and secondary schools, and this will mean there should be some new posts available. Nevertheless, you should try to keep abreast of changes in schools while you are not working so that you compete with newly trained teachers, who everyone says are better trained than ever before.

I want to work part-time now my family is growing up. I know about the problems of declining pupil numbers; will this make it harder to find part-time teaching posts?

It is difficult to be specific about what will happen to part-time posts in the future. On the one hand, falling rolls may lead to some schools axing part-time work in favour of full-time teachers. On the other hand, some schools may find they can no longer afford a full-time teacher but do have enough money for a fractional appointment.

What probably matters more is both what you have to offer to the school and how flexible you can be. If you only want to work Tuesday to Thursday and are never willing to help out on other days in a crisis, you will probably be less welcome than someone who can fit into the needs of the school. However, you should be warned not to let yourself become exploited. It is all too easy for part-time work to take over the whole week, so you effectively become full-time but are still paid as a part-timer, thus getting the worst of both worlds.

I completed a PGCE in secondary science in 1998, but have not taught since. How would I get back into teaching? Would I have to do a top-up course? If so, are there any I can complete while working full-time?

From the information you give in your question, it looks as if you successfully completed a PGCE but never entered teaching. This means that you won't have done your Induction Year. You are unlikely to find a tailor-made top-up course, but you could ask the Training and Development Agency for details of any courses that it is sponsoring in your area. As what you will need is probably to revisit skills such as classroom management, it is difficult to see how you can combine such a course with a full-time job, unless you can take the occasional day's leave as flexitime.

An alternative strategy would be to ask a school to devise a short training plan for you under the employment-based training programme. This should return you to the status of a newly qualified teacher relatively quickly. However, you would have to take a risk and give up your current full-time job.

I originally qualified in 1993 and taught for a year or two in a state school. During this period, I moved up a couple of spine points. However, for the past ten years I have been teaching English in a series of private schools. Where on the pay scale would it be reasonable for me to be placed on any return to the state sector?

There are provisions for cases such as yours in the Teachers' Pay and Conditions Document. Had you last taught in a maintained school before 1993, it would be up to the employer what salary to offer. However, as you have had some service since then, there are assimilation safeguarding criteria. These take account of the fact that the pay scales have been through several major revisions since you last taught in the state sector. If you were on point 2 when you left around 1995, you may still only be on the equivalent of M1 on the present scale. You can ask the school for extra discretionary points to cover your additional experience but, with no shortage of teachers of English across most of the country, and budgets tight, don't be surprised if you receive a distinctly lukewarm response.

For the past five years I have worked for an international school. I am now interested in going home to the United Kingdom to teach. What problems do you foresee? How best can I prepare myself?

You don't say how long you taught in the United Kingdom before going overseas. Also, have you taught the National Curriculum and International GCE or other types of curriculum while overseas? The problems you face are the same as those of UK teachers looking for jobs at present, but made worse by your probable inability to attend interviews easily.

Clearly, keeping in touch with what is happening in UK schools by reading the *TES* each week is a first step. Also, join a subject- or phase-based association to keep up to date. You could consider one of the distance learning MA courses for teachers in international schools. Ask your international school associations whether they will run seminars at INSET conferences on returning to teach in the United Kingdom. Apart from that, it means checking that your CV sells you effectively to the reader, who will be sceptical as to why they should employ you in preference to someone who has worked down the road. Your breadth of experience and knowledge of other cultures are valuable, but need selling to a head and governors who know little or nothing of the international school scene. You could try applying for jobs at an international school in London as a halfway house.

I am a British teacher but have been teaching overseas for the past five years. I want to move back to the United Kingdom and have a total of nine years' teaching under my belt. How much money could I expect to find in my pay packet each month? I think that my experience now puts me at M6.

The actual amount will depend upon whether you teach either in or around London or elsewhere in England or Wales. In central London you would be on a salary of £31,749, whereas in say, Newcastle, it would be £28,005 if you had been starting your job in September 2006. Don't forget that compared with teaching overseas, there is the added benefit of being able to join the Teachers' Pension Scheme. This is a generous index-linked scheme that is still tied to final salary. This is no mean benefit.

I wonder whether teachers seeking to return to teaching are less likely to be accepted because they are on UPS1. I know that some local schools only look for NQTs even though advertisements ask for teachers of all levels of experience.

This becomes an issue if you take a career break when you have reached the Upper Pay spine or are otherwise looking for a new job, perhaps because a partner has been relocated. Schools must re-employ you at no lower a basic salary than when you left. When there are plenty of teachers looking for work, as at present in many parts of the country, then this becomes an issue. Schools will seek the cheapest staff for basic classroom teaching, and only pay more for additional skills. So, if you leave on UPS2, as a basic classroom teacher with no additional responsibilities or expertise to sell to a potential employer, then you may well find it difficult to find another teaching post, especially if you were teaching in a 'good' school; you might find the only teaching posts are in more challenging schools. Heads who would once have offered you anything to teach at their school can now afford to be choosier. It's the law of the market.

I passed my NQT [newly qualified teacher] year one year ago and then went on to teach science at another secondary school. It was not a good experience; I became confused with where my career was going and left teaching in April 2005 after a period of stress-related absence. I find this all very embarrassing and am not sure how this reflects on me when applying for new teaching positions. I've now relocated and am missing being involved in teaching so much. The few questions that I have are:

1   As a secondary science teacher, am I allowed to do supply teaching in primary schools?
2   Are there any roles that I would be eligible for in a school that wouldn't involve teaching science 100 per cent of the time? I'd really like to take a more pastoral route, as this is definitely my forte, but am not sure whether I have to 'do more time' as a science teacher before I can move on to a role like this.
3   What non-teaching roles are there available for which you first need to have a teaching qualification in order to qualify?

I suppose what I'm saying is that I was such a good, caring, understanding, motivating influence while I was teaching (in a very difficult school) that the science teacher in me became less important and the pastoral side was the part that I really felt drawn to and found to be a more useful way to use my skills. I really want to get involved again but I don't want to be thrown into a demanding timetable again of the kind that destroyed me last time... and surely relaying these feelings to a potential employer would put them off me anyway?

Any advice would be greatly appreciated.

You pose an interesting question. Those entering teaching do so with a multitude of different talents and strengths. It is not clear whether you finished your Induction Year, as you say you left at Easter. If you didn't do so, then completing that would be a priority, as it provides the basis for you to move on. However, moving to a new part of the country may not make this easy. Nevertheless, don't assume, because you had a bad experience in a tough school, that all schools or departments are the same. It might be worth contacting the local authority to see whether there is a science adviser with whom you could discuss possible vacancies.

I do not think that doing supply work in a primary school would be a good idea. In most parts of the country there are now enough trained primary teachers looking for supply work, so that you might find that you were only employed in the most difficult schools and that might engender more stress.

Yes, do consider other pastoral-type posts. However, most schools would expect basic competence as a teacher, as you would be helping other teachers with problem youngsters. I suggest that you might like to undertake some career analysis to see what type of work really suits you and then consider whether some form of additional training might be necessary. In the meantime, you could consider tutoring on a one-to-one basis as a means of earning some income and still working with young people preparing for examinations. On a more formal basis, some local authorities employ staff to teach children who are out of school for whatever reason.

Good luck with whatever options you decide to pursue.

I am looking for advice on getting myself back up to speed. I have a PGCE (juniors) and had been teaching for five years when we moved to the United States. After ten years we are coming home and I want to get back in the classroom. For the past five years I have been working as an educational (teaching) assistant in an elementary school, so I do have more recent experience. Any ideas you have would be appreciated.

There are still some 'return to teaching' courses around, and one of these might be a useful way to update yourself to what has happened while you have been away. You could check with your local education authority to see if it knows of any such courses. The main change, as you will have noticed, is that jobs are not as plentiful as when you left. However, you should be able to make your experience work for you. You have an understanding of teamwork both as a professional and as an 'aide'. This should be a helpful selling point. With ten years of experience you could look for some more senior posts where the competition may be less fierce than for a basic classroom teacher post.

Until December 2004 I was a history teacher. I left to work in industry, but I am now considering returning to teaching. I generally enjoyed teaching but found the work extremely stressful. I am looking for advice: should I return to teaching? Is there an organisation that I could contact to help me deal with the stress levels and advise me how to deal with anger as the tiredness sets in?

You don't tell us why you are considering returning to teaching. Is this a positive decision or are you unable to find work in the industrial sector? Do not even think about returning unless you can honestly say you are returning for positive reasons, otherwise you will only quit again; your CV will start to look very patchy and you and your pupils will have had a miserable year. There is a teacher support line (http://www.teachersupport.info/) but if you think you need it before you return, this just confirms my view that teaching is probably not the career for you.

I taught in primary schools for eighteen years, but left five years ago to pursue other interests. I recently had six months off work with the beginnings of arthritis. I would like to return to education, possibly working within adult education in some form. What are my chances?

These days you need some experience before changing from primary teaching to helping adults learn. You may be able to offer work on basic skills courses, although helping adults who never mastered the basics in schools is not the same as working with young children. I don't know where you have been working for the past five year, but is there a need for trainers in that field? However, I think you need to check with your doctor about the prognosis for your arthritis. Any employer is likely to view this with some concern, and you cannot hide it on your application. You might want to contact your local further education college to see whether it has any suggestions about possible openings.

I retired from teaching two years ago but have discovered that I miss the job and the children. I am a fit and active 61-year-old. What are my chances of a part-time teaching job? How do I start looking? It is so long since I had to search for employment of any description.

It is nice to find someone still keen to teach at your age. Sadly, I think your chances will depend upon your experience and flexibility. There is a market for teaching posts and it is oversupplied with primary teachers, but still lacking some secondary teachers. Your best bet is to use your contacts in the local area to see what the job market is like for someone with your specific skills. You can register with agencies and local authorities but, given your age, they may not take you seriously. A personal recommendation would be much more useful. After all, it is only two years since you left full-time teaching, so you must still know some people who can help you in your search for a job. Good luck.

9   Job hunting

Some tips in dealing with the application process

APPLICATIONS

Can I apply online for jobs these days?

Although applying online is not yet common practice, more and more schools are including job application forms on their websites. The advantages of electronic applications are that you don't have to type out the same information every time. However, beware of using a standard letter of application; it should always be personalised to meet the requirements of each post you are applying for. Remember, however many posts you have applied for, this is the first time each individual school will have had anything to do with you.

Why do some schools ask for the letter of application to be handwritten?

This is a relic of the days before computers, when legible handwriting, both in the classroom and in reports to parents, was an essential requirement for teachers. These days, with IT taking over, I would have thought it was a much less important skill.

Should I always include my present head as one of my referees?

If you don't, then anyone reading your application is going to wonder why you haven't done so. If you have a good reason not to, then make it clear; don't leave the reader to play detective.

I have a criminal conviction for criminal damage, although committed when I was still at school. Should I mention it on my application form?

Yes, as it should be detected by the Criminal Records Bureau check. Owning up allows you to put it in context, especially if it is the type of offence that these days would only receive a fixed penalty rather than a visit to court. By completing your training and then working in schools you have demonstrated that the offence should already have been considered several times and not regarded as a barrier to your becoming a teacher. However, new rules to be introduced will tighten the regulations even further.

Teaching posts are scarce in the area where I want to teach. I have seen some jobs that I would like to apply for but am put off because I cannot offer everything that the school is seeking. What should I do?

Most schools create a wish list, some parts of which are essential and other parts are just desirable. For instance, I once saw an advert for a design and technology teacher that specified either textiles or electronics experience. Clearly, the school would be unlikely to find someone with both. When you send for the details, this should become apparent. However, if you think you can fulfil the main requirements for the post, but not all the subsidiary requirements, then I would still be inclined to apply, and make clear what else you have to offer. After all, nothing ventured, nothing gained.

Some schools offering posts say that a TLR [Teaching and Learning Responsibility supplement] will be available for a suitable applicant. Does this mean that they don't want a newly qualified teacher?

I am surprised that this practice hasn't been dropped after the recent staffing review schools carried out, but clearly it hasn't. If the post carries responsibility for teaching and learning, then it should say so. The new arrangements were supposed to stop schools using TLRs as a recruitment device; there are recruitment and retention points available for schools finding it difficult to make appointments.

INTERVIEWS

Can I ask to visit the school before the interview?

Much may depend upon how many applications a school is expecting to receive. For main-grade posts in areas where many applications may be received, it may just not be practicable. However, there is much that you can find out online these days about a school. Maybe someone on the *TES* Staffroom website (http://www.tes.co.uk/section/staffroom/) will be able to offer some opinions about the schools ...

I have been at my school for about eighteen months and am now looking for a new post. Will I be given time off for interviews?

Yes, you should be. Even if you are called for a number of interviews and aren't appointed each time, your school should just accept the situation. It might be a different case if they heard you were being offered posts and kept turning them down.

I don't feel that I do myself justice at interview. Is there anything I can do to improve my chances?

The first thing is to be prepared. Know why you are applying for this particular post, and think about how you would explain your interest to someone else. After all, if you reach the interview stage, you have passed the first test with flying colours and had your application form accepted as better than that of some other applicants. Remember, the first contact is a key one. Manner, bearing and tone of voice are even more important than the actual words you use. Most interview panels will start with an obvious question to help you settle down before testing your worth for the job. Be prepared to ask a question at the end, or, if your possible questions have been covered, say so, explaining what you would have asked about. There is value in arranging a mock interview with someone who knows you well and can be honest about where you might improve your technique.

What is the point of an interview? It doesn't tell the panel anything about my ability as a teacher.

This is one reason why schools ask for portfolios of work and even demonstration lessons. However, the traditional interview does allow a group of people to explore how candidates react to broadly similar questions. It also allows a dialogue to develop between interview and interviewee about specific issues and experiences, and helps to clarify what you have written on your application form. For more senior posts I would expect a school to use a range of techniques and not just a panel interview.

Do I have to accept the post immediately it is offered?

Assuming you have no need to discuss terms, such as salary or starting date, I don't see why you should not accept orally straight away. After all, that was surely the purpose of applying for the post in the first place. If you have any doubts that have arisen during the process, this is the time to raise them, and if they cannot be dispelled, then you would no doubt decline the post there and then.

WHAT CAN I EXPECT?

How much notice do I need to give when changing teaching jobs?

Generally for those who are not heads, it is two months if leaving at Christmas or Easter and three months if leaving in the summer. Some schools will allow you to leave earlier by mutual agreement.

When I had my interview I was led to believe that I would be teaching a particular timetable. On arrival I find myself assigned a less interesting timetable in an annexe that I didn't know anything about. What can I do?

You have a range of options depending upon how seriously you view the situation. At one extreme, if the advert and job description are nothing like what has materialised, you could threaten to quit. However, this is an extreme measure, and schools do have the right to change timetables as a result of changes in circumstances. It is to protect themselves against cases like this that teachers join professional associations. The school representative should be your first point of contact to discuss the situation. It may be that something can be negotiated. At the very least, you should be offered an explanation as to why the change has taken place. If you are genuinely not satisfied, then start looking for another job.

10 What does the future hold for teachers?

The next few years are likely to see some dramatic changes in the teaching profession. The historic Workload Agreement signed in early 2003 came into force over a period of three years starting from September 2003. It made considerable changes to what teachers were expected to do and what they can require others to do for them. Teachers in primary schools were more affected by some of the changes than teachers in the secondary sector. For instance, non-contact time had been common for many years in secondary schools but had rarely been available to those working in primary schools before the third stage of the Workload Agreement was introduced in 2005. This was followed at the end of 2005 by the switch from Management Points to payments for Teaching and Learning Responsibility (TLR) and the requirement that schools conduct a full review of their staffing structures to take account of the changes. Teaching is now a much more closely defined responsibility than it ever was in the past. However, anomalies still remain at the leadership level, with executive head teachers in danger of looking more like American school superintendents than leading teachers.

Two other factors that are likely to profoundly affect schools across the country over the coming few years are the continuing decline in the school population and the large number of teachers who will reach retirement age in the decade between 2006 and 2015. It has been calculated that nearly 40 per cent of the teaching force may retire in this ten-year period. Not only will this create the need for a large influx of newly trained teachers, even after the reduction in the school population is taken into account, but also many of those leaving will have been in the more senior positions.

The decade after 2006 will be a golden age for promotion opportunities for those who remain. It is not just that will there be many opportunities in schools, but there will be other career moves possible as the 'baby-boomers' of the 1960s and 1970s retire from the many other posts needed to ensure the education service works effectively.

However, there is no guarantee that schools will remain organised the way they have been for the past 130 years. The two by four by eight notion of education encompassed by the two pages of a book, the four walls of a classroom and the eight periods of the school day that still prevails in many schools would be almost instantly recognisable to the Victorian pioneers of state education. However, it may finally be challenged both by the state and by teachers.

Recent thinking by government has created more certainty about who a 'teacher' actually is, but has also expanded the numbers who work as a member of a learning team, with support staff and classroom assistants as well as qualified teachers now regarded as essential team members. How will the balance between the use of individuals, who are very expensive resources, and technology, which can be a cheaper alternative, be handled in the coming years?

In a world where self-employment is a growing phenomenon, why should teachers continue to be employees? It would be perfectly possible for groups of teachers to form 'practices' to sell their services to the education community. In doing so, they would take control of their own careers. This is a logical next step from the actions of those teachers who have signed on with supply agencies to avoid working in one school and to retain the freedom to choose when and how they will work. To be successful, such actions would require the teachers to mange their own professional development rather than relying on the decisions of others. The benefits might mean that a 'teacher' could combine the parts of the work he or she found attractive and avoid what was not congenial. If this work was necessary, the state would be forced to pay a higher price in the market to obtain the necessary services, as happens with salaries for head teachers at present, where supply and demand have a direct effect on the salary a school is prepared to offer a new head teacher.

What is clear is that those new teachers entering the profession in the middle part of the first decade of the twenty-first century will not end their working life until around the middle of the century. It is certain that the changes that they will encounter are difficult for many of us to comprehend. Forty years ago the telephone was not a universal household item; thirty years ago some schools still did not have a colour television; twenty years ago the BBC B computer had barely been invented and the PC was only just becoming available; ten years ago few of us had heard of the internet or text messages, and mobile phones were still like bricks. However, it is not only in the field of technology that changes have been apparent. Family structures have undergone huge change over the past few decades; organised religion has become less important for many, but a fundamental part of their lives for others; and affluence has made the global village a reality for many, while others still find a trip beyond their own community an adventure.

Education and educators, whether teachers, policymakers or consumers, will need to devise a structure that allows learning and education to take place in this evolving landscape; to do nothing will not be an option. Five years ago, CDs seemed the height of modern technology and had displaced both records and cassettes for recorded music. Now, downloading from the internet means that even CDs are on the way out, to join those other casualties of the electronic age, daisy wheel and dot matrix printers and floppy disks. More and more goods and services are being bought online. I don't know what will be the eBay moment for education, when the present system finally starts to fall apart. But it will come.

In responding to these changes, whatever form they take, teachers of today will need to be aware of how their own careers may be shaped. As professionals, the responsibility is theirs. My own journey has taken me from London to Oxford via Worcester and Durham. The journey has been from inner-city comprehensive to a teachers' centre and teacher training, from government adviser to businessman and journalist; and it isn't over yet. Partly the journey was planned, but partly it was a response to circumstances, both professional and personal. I never planned to become a teacher. Indeed, I only became one by accident, but happily it turned out to be the right choice. May your career be as rewarding and interesting as mine has been so far.

Appendix A

Analysis of number of advertised teaching posts in secondary schools

Table A.1 Analysis of number of posts in secondary schools advertised nationally between 1 September 2005 and 31 July 2006

Subject	Classroom teacher	Teacher with responsibility but not a head of department	Head of department	Total
Art & design	635	24	258	917
Business studies	388	29	159	576
Citizenship	49	7	33	89
Classics	29	2	10	41
Design & technology				0
General	852	141	302	1295
Graphic design	44	3	1	48
Home econ/food science	294	37	34	365
Resistant materials	105	9	2	116
Textiles	105	8	5	118
All design & technology	*1400*	*198*	*344*	*1942*
Dance	116	7	24	147
Drama	429	30	200	659
English	1882	446	494	2822
Expressive arts	12	1	40	53
General subjects	7	0	1	8
Geography	565	39	187	791
Health & social care	74	1	18	93
History	570	18	158	746
Humanities	189	37	141	367
IT	961	173	455	1589

Subject	Classroom teacher	Teacher with responsibility but not a head of department	Head of department	Total
Continued				
Law	20	0	0	20
Leisure & tourism	14	2	6	22
Modern foreign languages				0
French	294	10	31	335
German	79	3	17	99
Italian	3	1	0	4
Other languages	42	4	24	70
Spanish	107	10	29	146
General or combinations	520	70	239	829
All languages	*1043*	*98*	*340*	*1481*
Mathematics	1793	478	536	2807
Media studies	94	6	48	148
Music	535	36	297	868
Other subjects	114	26	158	298
Pastoral	8	17	388	413
Physical education	1317	223	321	1861
Performing arts	22	10	69	101
Personal & social development	88	6	55	149
Psychology	182	8	35	225
Religious education	675	77	277	1029
Sciences				0
Biology	190	13	82	285
Chemistry	196	14	82	292
Physics	229	18	79	326
General or combinations	1680	325	447	2452
Other sciences	18	7	5	30
All sciences	*2323*	*377*	*595*	*3295*
Social sciences	17	1	15	33
Sociology	61	2	16	79
Special needs	127	64	230	421
Vocational studies	12	7	46	65
Welsh	17	2	2	21
Total	**20526**	**7335**	**3125**	**30986**

The table is based upon an analysis of teaching posts advertised by maintained schools, plus academies, in the *Times Educational Supplement* and on leading websites for teaching. The table includes posts on the Main Scale and with no responsibility, those for classroom teachers with a responsibility payment but not heads of department and head of department posts on a TLR.

Appendix B

Salary scales from September 2006 to August 2007

Main Scale

Inner London	£23,577 – £32,820
Outer London	£22,554 – £31,674
London Fringe	£20,586 – £29,649
Rest of England and Wales	£19,641 – £28,707

Upper Pay spine

Inner London	£36,885 – £40,002
Outer London	£33,804 – £36,255
London Fringe	£32,043 – £34,389
Rest of England and Wales	£31,098 – £33,444

TLR 2

Anywhere between £2,306 and £5,689

TLR 1

Anywhere between £6,663 and £11,275
TLR points do not carry any regional adjustments

Leadership Scale

The scale is forty-three points in length. The range (Individual School Range, ISR) a post is advertised on depends upon factors such as the size of the school, the age of the pupils and the perceived difficulty in filling the post.

There are four scales covering the same areas as the main scale for teachers:

Inner London	£40,527 – £102,075
Outer London	£36,789 – £98,334
London Fringe	£35,025 – £96,576
Rest of England and Wales	£34,083 – £95,631

Appendix C

The projected future size of the school population

The projection of the changes in likely pupil numbers between 2003 and 2028 based upon the government's estimates of population changes is shown in Figure A.1.

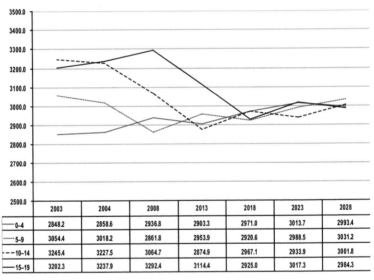

	2003	2004	2008	2013	2018	2023	2028
—— 0–4	2848.2	2858.6	2936.8	2903.3	2971.0	3013.7	2993.4
······ 5–9	3054.4	3018.2	2861.8	2953.9	2920.6	2988.5	3031.2
– – 10–14	3245.4	3227.5	3064.7	2874.9	2967.1	2933.9	3001.8
—— 15–19	3202.3	3237.9	3292.4	3114.4	2925.0	3017.3	2984.3

Figure A.1 Changes in likely pupil numbers by age, 2003–2028 (source: ONS England and GOR population, table 10)

Appendix D
Career paths for teachers

Some possible career paths for teachers are shown in Figures A.2 to A.6.

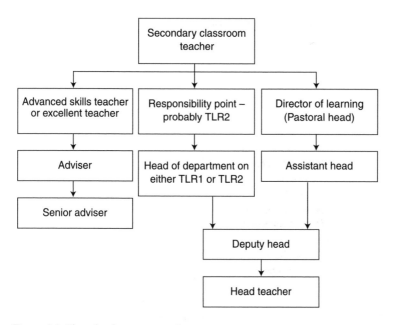

Figure A.2 The school route: secondary

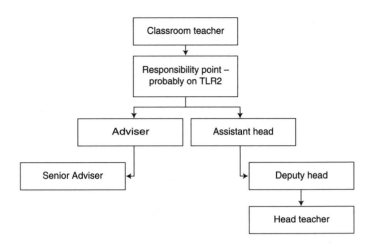

Figure A.3 The school route: primary

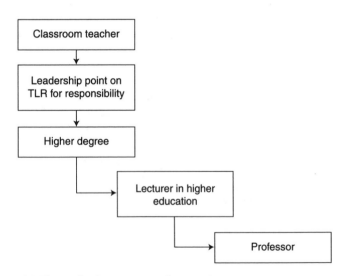

Figure A.4 The academic route: secondary or primary

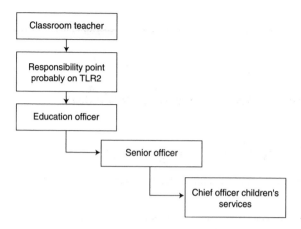

Figure A.5 The administrative route

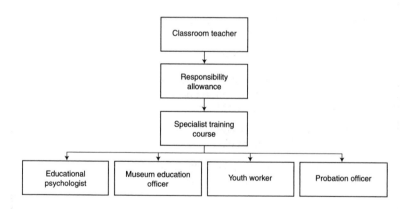

Figure A.6 The specialist route: some possibilities